Tim Bowden is a broadcaster, radio and television documentary maker, historian and author. Born in Hobart in 1937 (which means he is now quite old), he is well known for hosting the ABC-TV listener and viewer reaction program Backchat from 1986 to 1994.

He is the author of 17 books including *One Crowded Hour – Neil Davis, Combat Cameraman*; *The Way My Father Tells It - The Story of An Australian Life*; *Antarctica And Back In Sixty Days*, *Aunty's Jubilee – 50 years of ABC-TV*; *The Changi Camera* and *Stubborn Buggers* – the survivors of the infamous POW Outram Road gaol that made Changi look like heaven.

Bowden's background in journalism includes current affairs, news, and feature and documentary work. He has worked as a foreign correspondent in Asia (covering the Vietnam war) and in North America. In 1969 he was the first executive producer of the ABC radio current affairs program PM, before becoming a producer with the ground-breaking television current affairs program This Day Tonight in the early 1970s. In 1985 Bowden founded ABC Radio's Social History Unit. Since 1989 Tim Bowden has been actively broadcasting, writing and researching Australian activities in Antarctica. He was commissioned to write the official history of ANARE (Australian National Antarctic Research Expeditions) *The Silence Calling – Australians in Antarctica 1947-97.* Bowden also presented six half-hour documentaries Breaking the Ice on ABC-TV in 1996.

Tim Bowden received an Order of Australia for services to public broadcasting in June 1994. In May 1997 he was awarded an honorary degree of Doctor of Letters from the University of Tasmania.

Also available from ETT Imprint

by Tim Bowden

Ion Idriess: The Last Interview

No Plucking!

ROS BOWDEN

Trailblazer

TIM BOWDEN

ETT IMPRINT
Exile Bay

First published by ETT Imprint, Exile Bay in 2022

My thanks to my publisher, Tom Thompson, of ETT Imprint for his encouragement and professional advice on the publication of *Ros Bowden – Trailblazer.* I thank ABC Books for their permission to publish excerpts from the three books Ros Bowden wrote drawn from her interviews for the ABC: *Aspects of Nutrition* published in 1986, *Being Aboriginal – Comments, observations and stories from Aboriginal Australians*, published in 1990, and *Women of the Land – Stories of Australian Women* published in 1990. Thanks also to Allen & Unwin for permitting excerpts from my autobiography, *Spooling Through An Irreverent Memoir,* first published in 2003. TIM BOWDEN 2022

ETT IMPRINT
PO Box R1906
Royal Exchange NSW 1225
Australia

ISBN 978-1-922698-64-3 (paper)
ISBN 978-1-922698-65-0 (ebook)

Cover design by Tom Thompson
Design by Hanna Gotlieb

CONTENTS

Ros Bowden

Introduction

I had hoped to write this book in conjunction with Ros, but Alzheimers is a cruel disease, and I have had to attempt this book alone. We have been lucky enough to share half-a-century of joyous married life before the fog descended on her formerly sharp brain and feisty personality.

I hope our family, friends and a wider audience will enjoy this account of Ros' adventurous, well-lived life, and at least I will have the satisfaction of placing a copy of it in her hands even though she may not be able to fully comprehend it.

Tim Bowden

Father Eric and the newly arrived Ros, Ceylon. Baby Ros with her Nanny, Ceylon.

Ros in cockpit of crashed aircraft, Ceylon, with father Eric.

1

An Adventurous Start

Anne Rosalind Bowden was born on 15 December 1940 in Ceylon, and her parents, Eric and Margaret Geddes, did her no favours by registering her birth names in that order. Apparently they thought if they called their eldest daughter Rosalind Anne Geddes, the initials RAG might have caused her to be teased at school. But Anne has never existed except on formal documents. She has always been Ros, and if she was sitting waiting in a doctors' surgery and someone called out 'Anne' she invariably failed to respond.

Ros was born in Ceylon (now Sri Lanka) because her father Eric Geddes was a tea planter, and he married Margaret Bonney, from Sydney, after they met on a ship returning from England. Margaret, was the daughter of Mr Justice Reginald Schofield Bonney, who had been appointed a Supreme Court Judge of New South Wales in September 1940, with responsibilities for 'Exercising Matrimonial Clauses Jurisdiction', essentially the beginning of the State's first family court. He held that position until his death in 1950. He was admitted to the NSW Bar in 1907, and appointed a Kings Counsel in 1928.

Mr Justice Bonney often appeared before the High Court of Australia and in 1935 visited London where he once appeared before the Privy Council having been admitted to the English Bar. He married Lilian Butler in 1917, and they had three daughters, Helen, Margaret and Nora.

Ros told me that her mother Margaret had been offered the alternative of being given a coming out ball in London or use the money to have a skiing holiday in Europe. She chose the latter. It was on her return voyage to Australia that she met her future husband Eric, a tall, fair-haired manager of tea plantations. Eric had to disembark in Colombo while Margaret went on to Sydney. But they stayed in touch and as Ros recalled, 'My grandmother and my mother went to

Ceylon to look him over when their decision to get married was made – I don't think my grandfather was terribly pleased about that'!

They were eventually married in Australia, before heading back to Ceylon to start their lives together, announcing the arrival of the first of their three daughters, Ros, in December 1940. The family's circumstances changed dramatically when the Empire of Japan entered World War II on 27 September, 1940, by signing the Tripartite Pact with Germany and Italy, and invading French Indochina, though it wasn't until the attack on Pearl Harbor on 7 December 1941 that the United States of America entered the conflict.

But the Japanese first had their eyes on the British Eastern Fleet which was operating in the Indian Ocean, leading to the Easter Sunday Raid on Colombo by carrier-based aircraft of the Imperial Japanese Navy on 5 April 1942. The object was to destroy the Ceylon-based British Eastern Fleet thought to be in Colombo Harbour. But the British had advanced warning of this from their intelligence networks as early as March 1942, by pre-emptively dispersing its ships from Colombo Harbour before the attacks could take place. The Japanese Navy did not have radar at that stage, but the British Navy in Colombo did. Unfortunately it was switched off for maintenance when the Japanese bombers attacked Colombo Harbour!

By this stage, Eric Geddes had joined the British Army in Ceylon, and Ros' grandfather Reginald Bonney was well aware that his daughter, grandchild, and Margaret's companion, Ros' godmother, Sybil Morrison, were in a very dangerous situation. But how to get them out? Herbert Vere Evatt had been appointed a Justice of the High Court in 1930, but by 1940 had resigned from the High Court and returned to politics. By early October 1941 he had risen through Labor Party ranks to become the Minster for External affairs. Mr Justice Bonney knew Evatt through the law, of course, and contacted the new External Affairs Minister to see if he could pull some strings to get his stranded family back to Australia before a very likely Japanese invasion of Ceylon. Clearly the two men respected each other, but it was likely their politics were far apart. It seems that

Bonney had done some legal work for a growing fascist paramilitary organisation, the New Guard, which emerged from the Sydney-based Old Guard in 1931.

The New Guard became the largest and most successful fascist organisation in Australian history! It was known for its violent agitation against the Labor Premier Jack Lang, and was founded by Eric Campbell, a World War I veteran and former Old Guard member. At its peak the New Guard membership was estimated to be around 50,000, The followers were predominantly Anglo-Protestant, monarchist and anti-communist in nature.

The New Guard had its most successful publicity stunt on 19 March 1932 when Captain Francis de Groot, on horseback and brandishing a sword, managed to upstage Premier Jack Lang briefly by slashing the ribbon to pre-empt the official opening of the newly built Sydney Harbour Bridge. A paramilitary organisation it might have been, but its leadership was amateurish, ineffectual, and often compared with 'The Keystone Cops', and it faded away to insignificance three months after de Groot's clownish stunt.

It is not known whether Evatt knew of Bonney's possible connections with the New Guard, but Bonney was nine years older than the Minister for External Affairs, and their respect for each other was most probably linked to their careers in the law.

In any case, Evatt managed to arrange for Margaret Bonney, not-quite-two-years-old Ros and her godmother Sybil Morrison to be taken on board an Australian troop ship, which left Colombo Harbour the day before the Japanese bombers laid waste to Colombo Harbour. Port facilities were damaged, and ships in the harbour – and dispersed offshore – were sunk or damaged. The bulk of the British Eastern Fleet was not found, and survived. It relocated its main base to East Africa, from which it regularly deployed carrier task forces into the central and eastern Indian Ocean.

Ros, then not quite two-years old, has no memories of the journey to Australia of course, but it is likely that the troops were kind to an Australian toddler and her companions – the only females on the troop ship. It remained a great regret to Ros (who later in life had a distinguished career in recording oral history documentaries for ABC Radio) that she never asked her mother about that journey, which included a cross-continent railway trip on a troop train from Fremantle to Sydney, which cannot have been easy.

The Japanese did not invade Ceylon, and Eric Geddes stayed in Ceylon as a member of the British Army until the end of the war in 1945. In Sydney Ros and her mother Margaret moved into the large Bonney house, where Mr Justice Bonney clearly took much joy in the companionship of his refugee grandchild. There are photographs of him piggy-backing little Ros in the garden, and even sitting in her play pen with her, suffering the indignities of having his nose tweaked, even permitting little Ros to empty a wastepaper basket over his distinguished head. Reginald Bonney noticed Ros' devotion to her favourite dolls, which led to him writing a series of letters to her about the dolls' imagined lives. When it became clear that the Japanese forced had other problems to deal with apart from invading Ceylon, Margaret Geddes and Ros returned to Ceylon in 1943.

Ros remembers the voyage back to Ceylon as she used to roll around on the decks when the liner was ploughing through heavy seas. 'I didn't ever get seasick.'

On her return to Ceylon, then aged six, she was enrolled in a Catholic boarding school. 'There were a few of us there that weren't Catholics and I quite enjoyed it because I didn't have to wake up early and go to Mass.

'They used to have celebrations for the various Catholic Saints, and you had to walk about holding candles and so on, and I quite enjoyed that. I was there for about six months and then there was a place in a Protestant school and I was moved to there.'

It was rather boring just being at home, Ros recalled, just having a nanny and not much to do, so boarding school was a welcome change.

Back in Sydney, her grandfather, Reginald Bonney, began to write an account of the imagined adventures of her dolls he had sent her play with when she was in Sydney, and continued to write and post his stories to her in Ceylon until 1945, where they were read to Ros by her parents. These still exist, and were also typed up into a narrative by his youngest daughter Nora Bonney, who studied law but never practiced.

Nora Winifred Bonney had joined the Communist Party of Australia in 1939-1956. She was a rather small, shy and bespectacled young women who kept a low profile. This was useful when the Australian Secret Australian Intelligence Organisation, ASIO, raided the CPA headquarters in 1950, and Nora – then Secretary to the Communist Party Secretariat – quietly and unobtrusively gathered up the most sensitive and important files from the front office and hid them, while the ASIO operatives were strong-arming the other staff in the back rooms.

Meanwhile in 1943 Mr Justice Bonney had begun posting his letters to his granddaughter Rosalind in Ceylon to be read to her by her parents, detailing the imagined adventures of her favourite dolls.

Letter No. 1,
2 November 1943
My dear little Rosalind,

How I miss you. No one to help me in the garden or to ride on my back when I went to go about the house like an elephant; no one to have a nice little lump of brown sugar with at breakfast. I wish I could turn a somersault and come down the chimney while you were having breakfast. I'll bring you a nice little lump of brown sugar, or jump over the moon and land just where you are.

What fun it would be if I could do all sorts of things that can't be done, if I could change into a doll and come with you, but of course I can't change into a doll but I can't do all sorts of things, so I shall just have to tell you a story about a talking doll.

Once upon a time there was a talking doll, with a nice pink face and a real hat, white gloves and one red shoe and one blue shoe. The talking doll came along 'hoppity, hoppity, hoppity, hoppity, hop' first on her red shoe and then on her blue shoe and sat down between Rosalind and Topsy, the black doll.

'Hello', said the talking doll, 'What is your name? 'My name is Rosalind', said the little girl. And my name is Topsy', said the black doll. 'Tick-tock,' tick-tock said the talking doll, moving her head from side to side.

What a funny noise you make, said Rosalind. Grandfather has a watch that goes like that, and I didn't know that watches talked. 'They don't talk', replied the talking doll. 'They make a noise like that when they snore, and so do I when I snore. You see, Rosalind, I am a snoring doll as well as a talking doll. They wind me up when they want me to talk and most things that wind up go tick-tock tick-tock, don't they?'

'I don't know', said Topsy. 'Who told you to talk', said the talking doll? 'I did not talk, said Topsy, 'I only said I didn't know, surely that isn't talking, how can you talk if you don't know?' 'That is just your mistake, answered the talking doll, as she took her hat off and put it down hard on Topsy's head. 'The less you know the more you talk; it is all a matter of being wound up.'

Rosalind had never before heard Topsy talking. It seemed so strange, and the two dolls seemed so rude to each other that she almost wished they would be quiet for a while. Then she wondered whether the talking dog talking doll had a name because everybody who is anybody must have a name – or even two names and then you are somebody.

So Rosalind turned to the talking doll and ask her what her name was. 'Nobody', said the talking doll. 'But Nobody isn't a name, said Rosalind. 'Well well well well', said the talking doll. 'It must be a name because it is a name. It is my name when I am asleep, but when I wake up in the morning I have another name'.

'Oh dear', Rosalind thought, 'How funny, who would never of known that the dolly could have two names, one name in the morning and another name at night. I have two names, Anne Rosalind, but Mummy always calls me Rosalind. No one calls me Anne in the morning and Rosalind at night'.

'No', said the talking doll, 'No one has thought of doing that but they

could call you Anne in the morning and Rosalind at night if they only thought hard enough. I think of more things that people do; they wind me up like a clock and that makes me think what I am going to say, but they don't wind people up, so they can't think of things like that'.

Rosalind still thought it was very strange to have one name at night and another in the morning, so she asked the talking doll what her morning name was. 'Polly is my morning name', said the talking doll, 'and I'm going to sleep in your little bed tonight and wake up with you in the morning'. With that Polly said, 'tick-tock tick-tock', more and more sleepily, and went off to sleep like a good little doll.

When it seemed unlikely the Japanese would invade Sri Lanka, Ros and her mother had returned to what was still Ceylon in 1943, but in 1948 the island nation was granted independence by Britain to be known as the Dominion of Ceylon. (Dominion status within the British Commonwealth was retained until 1972 when on May 22 it became a republic and was renamed the Republic of Sri Lanka.)

On her return to Ceylon Ros had a wonderful adventure playground to enjoy. She played in the cockpits of crashed Japanese aircraft, had a shallow splashing pool in a thatched hut, and there are photos of her happily cooling off in it. There were Ceylonese nannies of course who came and went. In 1946, at the tender age of six, she was sent to boarding school, which she does not recall with any dismay, but enjoyed the communal life with kids of her own age, even though the food was pretty terrible and there was not enough of it. She found out later that her father Eric had also been put into boarding school at the same tender age. He was fourth generation Ceylonese-born and was sent to England to be educated as his forefathers had been.

In 1978 I suggested to Ros that a return to Sri Lanka would be a good thing to do. The best way to travel, we researched, was to hire a car and a driver. We flew in to Colombo and met our driver Pat Leanage, a middle-aged man whom we could not know then would become our on-going charity for the next twenty years. He of course spoke excellent English.

His first task was to work out where we wanted to go and what we wanted to see. Was it to be game parks, temples, beaches, national parks, the high country or what? We suggested to Pat that we were not interested in game parks, or beaches, and a few temples might be in order but not too many. We certainly wanted to go to the high country and tea plantations, and we did not want posh hotels, but had heard that traditional rest-houses were not only economical but historically interesting. We had a guide book so could suggest alternative attractions to Pat depending on where we were. Basically though, we wanted to eat the food of the country that Pat could recommend.

Sri Lanka has a convenient geography. The island is divided by a high mountain range, which conveniently has a monsoon alternating on one side for six months of the year. Sunshine and good weather is guaranteed on the non-monsoon side.

Although Sri Lanka was later to be wracked with conflict with the Tamil minority in the north of the island, we had arrived at a good time, but were advised that it would be best if we did not venture north of the harbour city of Trincomalee on the north-east coast of the island (which Ros particularly wanted to see).

We became very fond of the rest houses, with their traditional fans, verandahs, and open planning. These were the traditional places where the colonial English stayed during their inter-island travels, and I doubt if many survive today. We soon discovered that our driver Pat always chose the overnight stops where he got the best deal, but that did not worry us. We quickly liked the great variety of curries (always fried in coconut oil) and the local liquor Arrack distilled from the fermented sap of coconuts or sugar cane flowers. I recall asking Pat if it was permitted to take our own Arrack into the first rest house we stayed in, and he said he would ask.

We watched him walk to the front door and speak to the staff member there who shook his head. We were disappointed to see that and said so to Pat when he returned to the car. He looked bemused. 'But he said it would be just fine'! I had mistaken the curious sideways movements of the head from left to right of Sri Lankans (and Indians) signifying assent rather than no! We became aware that there were expensive bottles of Arrack which could be bought at liquor stores, but frankly we were extremely happy with the local moonshine.

The capital of Sri Lanka, Kandy, is situated appropriately close to the centre of the tear-drop shaped island nation. We took in some temples and reclining Buddhas before heading north to the central province of Matale intrigued to visit Sigiri Rock, also known as the Lion Fortress. This spectacular rock fortress, at 180 metres, dominates its surrounding countryside. An enormous carved lion greets visitors halfway up the rock on a small plateau, said to perform a dual role – to greet visitors and warn enemies. Those who brave the complete time climb and reach the top find an amazing patchwork of raised gardens after passing fascinating frescoes and graffiti – which we did not see at the time, but only in an aerial photo later. It was established 1500 years ago as the stronghold of a rogue king – which did not save him – but remains to this day one of the earliest and best-preserved examples of ancient urban planning.

By this time we had started to climb over the central mountain range, which had our driver Pat often leaving the car without explanation. He eventually told us he was offering up prayers to the Gods for our save travel in this challenging terrain! We hoped his prayers related to robust brake pads in our vehicle.

While we were in the high country we asked Pat to find the tea estate which her father Eric had managed when Ros was born. Unusually this estate ranged from high, though middle and down to low country which was a rare happening. When we located it, we had been unable to get a message through announcing our arrival. We drove to the main homestead, which Ros was delighted to find unchanged from her early memories, complete with a large portico covered in ancient climbing flowering vines.

The current owners, Mr and Mrs de Silva, seemed pleased to see us, invited us to morning tea, and even located an old clerk who remembered Ros as a little girl. The de Silvas told us that they tried to maintain the homestead as a historic property, which they had managed superbly.

It was a terrific holiday, and not long after the security situation with the Tamil's in the north deteriorated, and it would not have been safe for us to travel even to the port city of Tricomalee in the north east.

We enjoyed our time with Pat Leanage, but it was not long before his begging letters began. I think the first one was to buy him some new spectacles, which cost some $300 Australian dollars, which he needed to keep working as a driver. Then there were school fees for his children, and a myriad of other needs. This went on for about twenty years and God knows how many thousands of dollars. Eventually one of his sons emigrated to Australia with HIS children and we decided to hand over to him to help out his Dad. Still he had been our personal charity, and we had probably been able to give him a higher standard of living during that time.

When World War II ended, Eric Geddes had to return to England to be demobbed, and Margaret and four-year-old Ros went with him. They stayed for a time with Eric's sister Elaine in Exeter, Devon, in 1946. Ros started school there and her sister Julia was born there on 29 October. They all found England very cold, and Eric, who had not been able to find a suitable job decided to take Margaret and their two girls to Australia in late 1946.

In 1948 the newly independent Ceylon began to get rid of Europeans, and in 1949 Eric Geddes decided to take up a tea-planting manager's job in South India (despite his ancestral connections with Ceylon), and moved his family to Ootacamund (known colloquially as Ooty) in the Nigiri district of the State of Tamil Nadu. At 2,240 metres, its cool climate made it a popular summer holiday destination in Southern India, and ideal for growing tea. Ros was seven when this move was made although she was eight before the end of the year as her birthday was in December.

So began an exciting period of her young life with considerable freedom to roam about the high country near the family homestead. She was well aware of dangers lurking in the surrounding jungle, and evolved her own unique methods of dealing with them. Elephants roamed free in the district and Ros always carried a mouth organ when she went out. She knew that elephants, being very large animals, would find it difficult to chase her if she ran in a zig-zag pattern, at the same time playing her mouth organ to further confuse the charging pachyderm known not to like music. Fortunately this was never put to the test.

There were also panthers to be feared. Ros' unique plan to save herself from a panther leaping down from a jungle tree was to always carry a box of matches (as well as the mouth organ) so that if a panther did leap on her she would set fire to the soft hairs under its belly to dissuade it from taking any further interest in her. Again, this happily remained theoretical, although on one occasion when she was walking by herself in the jungle, everything suddenly went very quiet. She looked up to see a panther sprawled along the limb of an overhanging tree and thought it best to be on her way.

Now eight years old, she was enrolled in another boarding school at Ootacamund which she enjoyed as she had even at the tender age of six in Ceylon.

Ros enjoyed her holidays on the tea estate, and spent quite a lot of her time with the servants. One of her nannies used to take her down to the kitchen where she was friendly with the cook. There Ros remembers she was encouraged to stretch out her hand and hold the cook's penis. Things did not progress to anything more serious, Ros remembered, except being asked to hold the cook's cock rather puzzled her at the time. 'I wasn't really very interested, but that's what I was asked to do and my nanny and I guess the cook, probably liked me to do that.'

She was allowed to roam the higher country near the house on her own, and used to delight in setting fire to patches of lemon-grass (with the matches reserved for an attacking panther) and watching the flames move slowly up the hill. Curiously no one ever stopped her doing this.

Ros liked to smoke in the afternoons. 'I used to pinch cigarettes from the round tins about the house. I think I gave some of these to the servants, but I did smoke them a bit'.

As a toddler her youngest sister Jane recalls Ros taking her and her middle sister Julia and one of the nannies up into the hill country behind the homestead, but when the nearby jungle became strangely quiet with no bird calls, Ros sensed danger and they all beat a hasty retreat back to the house.

There were only about five boys at Ros' boarding school, who had to learn to play cricket before heading off to their expensive Public Schools in England. (Why the British referred to their private schools as 'Public' remains an enduring mystery.)

Ros' nascent feminism came to the fore when she discovered that the boys were the only ones chosen to bat and bowl, while the girls were deployed around the wicket do the fielding for them. Although Ros' enthusiasm for cricket then and now remains at a level of the interest a dog might evince in a plate of lettuce, but she was unhappy about the unfairness of this situation. She went to her Headmistress and said that either the girls should bat and bowl too, or the boys could play netball. The Headmistress agreed, and everyone involved batted, bowled, and fielded.

Then came handicrafts. Again, the girls were expected to mend sheets and service the boys by darning their socks. Ros presented herself to her Headmistress again (who was obviously by the standards of the day a progressive woman) and said she would rather do carpentry. This was also agreed to.

(In later life after we married I was very glad Ros HAD learned carpentry, because I was hopeless in that area, and Ros was able to put together the flat-packs of furniture ordered from IKEA. A flat we once owned in Lane Cove, Sydney, was a virtual shrine to IKEA, as was the early occupancy of our beach house we had built at Boomerang Beach on the Mid North Coast of NSW in 1979 before moving there permanently from

Ros in Sydney after evacuation from Ceylon piggie-backed by her long-suffering grandfather Mr Justice Reginald Bonney.

Ros nursing her youngest sister Jane, as Julia holds her doll in India 1948.

Ariel view of Sigiri Rock showing garden plots.

our house in Northbridge in 2000 which we sold – also enabling our two adult sons to leave home. Three weeks before the new owners were due to move in Barnaby had still not cleaned out his upstairs room. Ros and I though he probably hoped the new owners would let him stay… I did make sure he moved his pot (literally) plants where he had hidden them on the roof tiles near the chimney.

By 1952 it was decided that Margaret would return to Sydney with her three daughters, while Eric continued with his management of the tea estate.

Jane, who was only three, remembers crying when she left India, as she had been very close to her nanny. The ship was like a big adventure playground, and Jane remembers talking with her sister Julia through the ship's ventilators on the upper deck. Although only three, Jane remembers the dinners at night with exquisitely set tables with white-tablecloths, napkins, silver tableware as stewards in white uniforms and gloves, brought the different courses to table. Eric and Margaret dressed formally for these occasions.

While Margaret and her two younger sisters returned to India in 1952, Ros stayed with her mother's eldest sister Helen Treatt and her husband Frank in Sydney. They had two daughters, but this was not a success as Ros did not get on well with her younger cousin, and because of that was enrolled as a boarder at Abbottsleigh School, in the northern Sydney suburb of Wahroonga in 1953, then aged 12. Ros was happy about this.

By the end of that year things had become impossible for Europeans on the tea plantations in India, and Eric and Margaret and Ros' two sisters returned to Australia at the end of 1953. They went straight to Tasmania, after a brief phone call to Ros from the airport on their way through. Ros joined them by the end of that year, and flew directly from Sydney Harbour to Hobart by flying boat, landing on the River Derwent, which was an exciting way to travel then.

Ros was enrolled as a day student at the Fahan School in the suburb of Sandy Bay, which was only a short bus trip from where Eric and Margaret and Ros' two sisters were living in the southern suburb of Taroona.

Penny Ford, who lived near the Geddes' at Taroona, recalls Ros starting at Fahan at the beginning of 1954 when they were both 14, 'It was a difficult time to start when secondary school friendships had already been well established. And, of course, Ros didn't want to be there having been moved on from Abbotsleigh in Sydney.'

When Penny first met Ros she thought her exotic, with her red hair and Ceylonese citizenship. They used to catch the bus to Fahan School along with Robin Nevin, destined for a stellar theatrical career in later life.

The house Eric and Margaret Geddes had rented was a flat-roofed white painted house positioned in the middle of a large lawn, looking as though it had just pushed its way up through the grass overnight like a mushroom.

Penny remembers visiting this house and meeting Ros' younger sisters, Julia (who had blonde hair and resembled her father) and Jane who was skinny and red-headed. 'I was slightly bemused by her parents who seemed remote from every-day life, and certainly gave Ros a great deal of freedom – I guess she had to be very self-reliant with all the many moves she had in her life.'

Compulsory military training for young Australians was reintroduced in 1951 by the Liberal and Country Party alliance Government. It was the third such scheme to have existed in Australia since Federation. Eighteen-year-old men were required to undertake 176 days of military training as part of the National Service scheme. In 1957, I was a part-time student at the University of Tasmania, so instead of doing three months basic training, to be followed by two years in the Citizen Military Forces (CMF), university students were allowed to do two months basic training in their vacation, during January and February. However this would be followed by three years in the CMF.

I shed my blood for my country in Brighton Camp to the north of Hobart.

One compelling reason to celebrate the end of my national service training in 1957 was that I was deeply smitten. I met petite and dark-haired Penny Ford at a party, and she seemed to like me to. She was was three years younger than me and in her last year at Fahan School, but that seemed unimportant. We managed to see a lot of each other as the year went on. Fortunately her mother Marjorie did not seem too dismayed by this older journalist taking out her eldest daughter, and often produced a sherry decanter when I called. I did get some mild ribbing from my fellow journalist cadets for dating a schoolgirl, but that ceased as soon as they met Penny. Penny's best friend was Ros Geddes, who had started at the Fahan School three years earlier. I quickly found out she had been born in Ceylon and had lived there and in Southern India. (She could swear in fluent Tamil – a good party trick).

To the dismay of the two maiden ladies who ran the Fahan school, the Misses Morphett and Travers, Ros decided to leave after passing her Higher School Certificate and get a job. She was a bright student and 'Mops' and 'Trav' (as they were known at Fahan) even offered to waive her school fees for the next year so she could Matriculate, but Ros was adamant. Her parents were not well off, or coping all that well with non-colonial life and her two younger sisters were still at school.

Ros saved enough money from her job with the AMP to buy a 1929 Willys car. It was was a singular vehicle. The interior was in bad shape, so Ros pulled out all the tatty inner lining of the roof and sides and painted it the interior bright pink. She then pasted a collage of colour pictures cut from magazines over the pink inside of the roof. Like an Army Blitz Wagon the Willys did not have synchromeshed gears, double de-clutching was essential. Ros had not mastered this technique. She needed to get a driving license, after I taught her to drive. On the day of the license test, Penny sat in the back seat of the Willys charming the young policeman assigned to the test. I sat in the front surreptitiously double-declutching for Ros with my right foot on the clutch pedal. We all had a lot of fun, and when we got back to the police station, the constable reluctantly left the back seat and Penny's charms and awarded Ros her license. (She had actually knocked the witches hats over in demonstrating her non-ability to back into a parking space). The young policeman approved her licence but then said, 'Now go away and learn to drive'. Ros loved her Willys car, but no one told her about putting oil in the differential, so the transmission seized up terminally a few weeks later. Alas, Ros couldn't afford to have it fixed.

In 1955, the year I left school, I successfully applied for a cadetship at the Hobart Mercury to enter journalism. Because most kids in those days did what their parents wanted them to do, my father was particularly keen for me to get a university degree from the University of Tasmania. This meant a part-time course, where at two subjects a year, it would take me five years to get my Bachelor of Arts degree, which stretched ahead like eternity. I couldn't really be a proper university student, but just visited the campus to attend lectures.

In the meantime Penny Ford had transferred her affections to someone else (rather gallingly a fellow cadet at the Mercury, Douglas Blain). Ros Geddes and I continued to be friends, but did not really see much of each other. When 1960 rolled along and I donned a hired academic gown and a square hat with a tassle and picked up my degree at a ceremony in the Hobart Town Hall, I couldn't wait to leave Tasmania for overseas. Many of my friends had done this, and I set sail on an Italian liner, the Neptunia bound for Genoa, a wonderful five-week voyage with stops at exotic ports like Singapore, Jakarta, Cochin in India, Aden – through the Suez Canal – to Port Said, and further days at Messina, Naples and finishing at Genoa. I bought a Vespa motor scooter there and headed off over the Brenner Pass (no tunnel in those days) through Switzerland and France and a ferry across the English Channel to Dover and on to Cambridge where my Uncle Philip was a Don there (he was also a Fellow of the Royal Society through his pioneering work in researching the friction between metals) and had a house at the Backs where he and his wife Margo lived with their four children. The eldest boy, Piers, was already following in his father's footsteps at Cambridge.

They generously put me up for some weeks until I borrowed fifty pounds from Uncle Philip, and like Dick Whittington, took off to seek my fortune in London. Well the fortune eluded me, but I did find work with the BBC General Overseas Service (later the World Service) as a freelance interviewer. The BBC paid five guineas for each accepted assignment, which covered a week's rent in my Hampstead bed sitter, another interview meant I could eat, a third paid for drinks, and the rest was gravy. (I did manage to pay back the fifty pounds borrowed from Uncle Philip).

I managed to save enough to pay for holidays in Europe, travelling on my Vespa, and headed for the warmer climes in France, Spain and Italy. I had not forgotten Ros and used to send her postcards from exotic locations. On one holiday I joined up with the Bowden family in Switzerland and was inveigled into a rock climb with my cousins which scared the bejeezus out of me. We had a Swiss guide who was not impressed by my rock-climbing abilities and kept calling me a 'crapaud' which means 'toad' in French. I noticed that instead of clinging by our fingertips to rocky crevices I saw there was an easier route quite near our climb. I pointed this out and was greeted with even greater scorn by the guide. To my mounting (as it were) horror I realised that rock climbers always chose the most difficult and challenging way to the top! My mountain climbing in Tasmania had always been designed around taking the easiest route to the summit.

When we did reach the highest point I sought solace from a Spanish wine-skin carried in my back-pack, imbibing red wine for some Dutch courage to face the equally perilous descent – in some ways more scary than the way up.

I sent a photo of me holding up and drinking from the wineskin on the summit to Ros Geddes, (who had moved to Sydney and was training to be a nurse) with a letter detailing my ordeal as a wannabe rock-climber with no safety ropes. I continued to send cards and letters to her for the next two-and-a-half years. At that stage the BBC offered me a job as a producer, but I was not interested in becoming an expatriate like many other Australians were doing at the time. I was homesick for Tasmania (my Aunt Dorothy used to send me dried gum leaves every Christmas so I could burn them and take solace from the pungent eucalyptus smoke). I also managed to get a free passage home on a cargo ship.

Television had just come to Tasmania, and I applied for the job of Talks Officer Launceston which meant I contributed to Radio Current Affairs and fledgling occasional contributions to television. The then Supervisor of Talks, Anthony Rendell (who in bygone days had introduced me to the mysteries of portable recorders and editing quarter-inch magnetic tape with scissors and sticky tape) had come up with a very good idea to start a weekly television current affairs program which he unfortunately called Week. (You can imagine what the announcers did with that: 'For another Week program listen at the same time next week'.)

Without much hope, or so I thought, I applied for the job of Talks Officer in Singapore in early 1965. Only three overseas positions belonged to Current Affairs Radio, the other two being London and New York. To my surprise I got the job and prepared to head off to South-east Asia to be a foreign correspondent. Bill Peach, whom I had got to know in London when he was seconded by the ABC for a year with the BBC General Overseas Service, was now back in Sydney and said he would throw a party for me on my way to Singapore. Was there anyone I might like him to ask to this farewell occasion. I said 'Ros Geddes' who was then working as a registered nurse at Prince Alfred Hospital. I hadn't seen Ros since I headed off to England in 1960. It was good to see Ros again, and although I did not realise at the time, she had started to see me with fresh eyes. I only recently found out from one of her school friends who happened to be in Sydney at that time, Diana Payne, that Ros told her after Bill's party, that she planned to travel to Singapore to 'capture' me! Although, as will be revealed, that proved to be more difficult than might have been imagined.

Postcard sent to Ros in 1961 of me imbibing some Dutch courage from a Spanish wineskin after having reached the summit of a rock-climbing ascent of a Swiss mountain. (Right) Sister Ros Geddes as a newly fledged trained nurse.

From left: Me, Ros and Tasmanian cameraman Neil Davis in Singapore 1966.

2

Getting Together With Ros

There could not have been a better time to be sent to South-east Asia as a foreign correspondent. In 1965 the Menzies inspired fantasy that Australia was somehow linked to Britain by some kind of spiritual – and economic – umbilical cord was being replaced by a belated but timely awareness that we had better take account where we actually lived. The Vietnam War was hotting up with President Johnson pumping in half a million US troops to keep the 'Commies' at bay, and President Sukarno's declaration of a war of confrontation (*Konfrontasi*) in 1963 against the newly federated Malaysia – which he regarded as a neo-colonialist plot – and Malaysian, Australian and British troops in battle against Indonesians in the former British Borneo, now Sarawak and Sabah. Despite the sideshow of *Konfrontasi,* the British were preparing to leave their former colonies of Singapore and Malaysa to decide their own regional destinies.

As far as newsgathering in Asia was concerned, the ABC was ahead of its time. When I took off from Sydney airport in a Qantas Boeing 707 in some style (even humble public servants like myself travelled first-class overseas until Gough Whitlam ended all that in1972), the ABC had permanent correspondents in Tokyo, Jakarta, New Delhi, Saigon, Kuala Lumpur and Singapore – where the ABC's South-east Asian office was located. We also had stringers in major centres like Manila, Bangkok and Hong Kong. China was shut to western correspondents in the time of Chairman Mao.

Such was the hunger for news from the region that what Prime Minister Lee Kuan Yew said in Singapore that day would make it onto an Australian domestic news bulletins, as well as Radio Australia. (Conversely, Singaporeans couldn't have cared less about what was happening in Australia as I was to discover quite quickly.)

The ABC News Department (which controlled the ABC's overseas news gathering) regarded Talks Department officers as arty-farty types certainly not to be trusted to report hard news, but because I was a 'proper' D grade journalist – thanks to the *Mercury* – I was allowed to file for News as well as Talks current affairs.

It was early evening when my Qantas flight touched down at Paya Lebar Airport on Singapore Island, and as the door swung open, I breathed in the heady, humid, spicy – slightly crutchy – scent of rotting vegetation and a whiff of cloves from *kretek* cigarettes. I was twenty-eight years of age, single, and I couldn't believe my luck at scoring this assignment and I felt, correctly as it turned out, that I was on the brink of adventures that could hardly be imagined.

My fellow Tasmanian, Sydney cameraman Neil Davis, had precisely those feelings when he landed at the same airport a year before to work for Visnews, the international news-film arm of Reuters Newsagency. He, as I, marvelled at the sight of people virtually living on the streets in the benign balm of the tropics, patronising the pavement street stalls, eyes flashing, burnished skin shining under the pressure lamps of the outdoor markets, and the animated chatter in Cantonese, Malay and English. Neil had based himself in Singapore as the Indo China war quickly became the world's biggest on-going story, and I was looking forward to meeting up with him again.

It was alleged by some of my colleagues there was a kind of Tasmanian Mafia at work in the ABCs Asian operations. Davis (who worked administratively to the ABC's Singapore office) was already filming action in the region, Philip Koch (another refugee from the *Mercury*) was in Jakarta and Tony Cane (from the ABC in Hobart) was about to be posted to New Delhi. Now I had arrived to swell the Tasmanian ranks and further fuel the allegations.

There had been a changing of the guard in the ABC Singapore office, and not before time. The previous Representative, Ted Shaw, was a Walter Mitty character claimed in his cups – where he was most of the time – to have broken wild brumbies in far north Queensland, played test cricket for

Australia and to have interviewed Adolf Hitler in Berchesgaden before the war – all about the same time. 'Eva Braun was with him the second time I saw him. You could see a woman's touch – the curtains had changed'. Ted, like all good liars was never short on descriptive detail to flesh out his fantasies. He seldom went anywhere but his favourite local bar to perve on the ample mammaries of the barmaid he called 'Titty Lim', and explained his absences from the office by saying he was at Phoenix Park, where British military intelligence was located and which he almost certainly never visited. He had been appointed by the previous ABC General Manager, Sir Charles Moses, whom he managed to entertain so well every time he came through Singapore that any discrepancies and Shaw's ramshackle operation were overlooked. He had enormous *chutzpah.*

Neil Davis loved outrageous characters and was fascinated by Ted's wild and ingenious stories – but he spent most of his time away from Singapore and only had to have fleeting contact with him. Hitler's interlocutor and wild brumby-buster wasn't able to charm his new boss, Talbot Duckmanton, who didn't share Moses penchant for heavy boozing, and unsportingly had ABC accountants take a close look at the books. Shaw had been recalled to Sydney by the time I arrived.

The new Singapore representative was Peter Hollinshead, who had just turned forty – a forceful journalist from the stable of the ABC's News department. His wife, a big, gregarious blonde who in her day had marched with the surf lifesaving flag along Coogee beach, quickly became known to the correspondents in the region as Mother Asia. Peter was the antithesis of Ted Shaw. He was a straight talking, competent newsman, fiercely loyal to his staff and expecting nothing less in return.

The ABC office was in a rather dilapidated three-story building at 302 Orchard Road, just across from the smart, newly-built Indonesian Embassy, unoccupied due to President Sukarno's *Konfrontasi* with Malaysia. There were still empty building blocks covered in *lalang* grass on Orchard Road in the mid 1960s, now the high-rise heart of Singapore's premier shopping and business district. Our building had some eight local staff, including the driver of Peter Hollinshed's official black Holden car.

Omar, a skinny Malay of indeterminate age, who sported of the worst fitting pair of false clappers with bright orange gums it is ever been my experience to see. We always meant to club together to buy him some better dentures, but never got around to it. It had a small studio of sorts with soundproofing and some rundown tape recorders and switching gear presided over by our technician, Lee Kim Chwee. Peter (a dreadful man in bestowing enduring nicknames) immediately dubbed Kim Chwee 'Carrier' because of his insistent calls of 'Hello Carrier' when he was trying to get through to Singapore Telecom to access a broadcast line to Sydney.

Singapore was a wonderfully exciting place then and was yet to experience the spectacular development which transformed it into the ordered controlled metropolis of today. You had to step carefully to avoid falling into deep and malodorous concrete monsoon rains. Pavements were cluttered with *makan* carts (mobile food stalls) selling everything from noodles to turtle soup served in the luckless creatures' own shells. As soon as the sun set, the Orchard Road market set up with pressure lamps blazing under temporary awnings, displaying tropical fruits and vegetables, cooking utensils, ceramics, hardware, clothes and vinyl records of Chinese popular songs. Chinatown was an exotic place to visit, with crowded shop houses and stained walls, their cracks spouting tufts of grass and optimistic tree seedlings. Coffee makers worked alongside tin-smiths and pavement cobblers, while the click clack of wooden clogs on the paving stones seemed in syncopation with the buskers sawing away on single-string Chinese violins. Small boys ran among the crowds with tin trays carrying glasses of fragrant Chinese tea and wizened old grand-mothers in traditional dress shepherded their button-eyed grandchildren through the chaos. Before the bulldozers had completely cleared nearby Chinatown all away in the 1970s, a survey was done asking tourist what they most wanted to see in Singapore. Chinatown was near the top of the list. The clearance went on as high-rise flats took place of the old shop houses. The Singapore authorities simply said, ' Why should our people live in squalor'? They had a point. Colourful it may have been, but hardly sanitary. But it was the smelly, vibrant, raffish Singapore I knew and loved in the mid 1960s.

I was soon travelling to where the action was in nearby countries, Borneo, Indonesia, Thailand, Laos and South Vietnam where the civil war was intensifying with President Johnson sending half a million troops ostensibly to help the struggling South Vietnamese Army (ARVN) combat the invading Communist troops from the northern half of their divided country.

Early in 1966 I had an unexpected and extremely pleasant surprise when Rosalind Geddes arrived in Singapore. By now a fully-fledged nursing sister, she had resigned from her job at the Prince Alfred hospital in Sydney and decided to head to Singapore where she hoped to get a job. I met her ship and arranged accommodation at the York Hotel a rather charming old colonial-style hostelry. Ros was a tropical girl, having been born in Ceylon.

There was no guarantee of work in Singapore, but Ros was hopeful of getting a nursing job in the privately run Gleneagles Hospital which would also ensure her a work permit. She lived in the York Hotel for a month hoping a job would turn up and loved living in Singapore. We saw a lot of each other. One scented evening, under the slowly turning ceiling fans of her York Hotel room, we put our relationship on a less platonic basis. It was high time for both of us. More than a decade had passed we first met. Long-term friendship had blossomed into love.

When 'my colleague' Don Simmons came to Singapore on leave from Saigon he was courting, petite, blonde Kim Dwyer, who was working as a nanny for the Australian ambassador's children in Saigon. Kim's parents were also with the Department of External Affairs, which is I suppose how she came to be there. One sunny Singapore morning I picked up Don in my newly acquired car – a rather sporty Vauxhall Brabham Viva, the first new car I had ever owned – or more accurately began to pay off on hire-purchase, and called by the York Hotel to pick up Ros. She saw us waved cheerily and began to walk towards the car. Simmo was a perceptive fellow, and there was something about her body language that attracted his attention. He turned to me and said, 'You're fucking that woman!' I said it was none of his business. 'You are, you bastard, I know you are'!

Ros scored a vacancy at Gleneagles Hospital which gave her a salary plus the essential work permit. She moved into nurses' quarters at the back of the hospital which made intimacy more difficult, but not impossible. There was always my flat at 11F Jalan Jintan. We developed the habit of driving down into the city on Saturdays to have a curry lunch at a Muslim restaurant called the *Majeed*, which not only served brilliant curries, but wonderful *roti* – a delicious offering which began as a small ball of dough and then was rolled and skilfully flung out by the chef as a kind of shawl, until it was either wrapped around a raw egg or savoury mince, and cooked on a hotplate sprinkled with oil. Singapore Indian Muslims were relaxed about Australian unbelievers drinking alcohol on the premises and cheerfully sent out small boys to bring back large cold bottles of Tiger beer. After our exotic lunch we would return to Jalan Jintan to make post-prandial love under my lazily turning bedroom fans. They were wonderful days.

Regretfully the ABC kept sending me away from Singapore on assignments. It was something to do with my being a foreign correspondent. Ros got more use out of my shiny white new Vauxhall Brabham Viva car that I did.

The terms and conditions of my arduous tropical service (the ABC overseas staff worked under the Department of External Affairs guidelines) gave me home leave once a year as well as two weeks in the Cameron Highlands of Malaya. This was a colonial hangover from the days before air conditioning when toiling public servants were permitted a break in the 'high country' to play golf and recharge there their exhausted personal batteries. It was not however, compulsory. You could take the equivalent of the return train fare and go somewhere else. I did not regard Singapore is a hardship post, which was how it was officially categorised. Frankly, to quote the former British Prime Minister Harold Macmillan, 'I'd never had it so good'.

I flew home to Tasmania on leave (first class in those days) to enjoy a Christmas with the Bowden clan at the family weekender on the east coast of southern Tasmania. With consummate journalistic timing I flew out of Hobart the day before the 7 February bushfires in 1967 – among the most disastrous ever to strike our bushfire-prone continent. A lethal combination of high temperatures and tempestuous winds as high as 80 km/h swept the fire down from the forests on the flanks of Mount Wellington within two kilometres of the centre of Hobart. At the peak of the disaster the hot winds blew many of the fires together so they destroyed everything they touched. In some places the temperatures were so high the bitumen on the roads melted and burst into flames. Rogue wind gusts carried the fire from exploding gumtrees – and houses – five kilometres in a few seconds. One survivor said, 'It was as though the wind was on fire'.

Firefighters could do little because of the scale of unpredictability of both the wind and fires. Some windows in brick houses simply exploded (or imploded) before the actual flames reach them, while timber houses nearby were untouched. At Middleton, a coastal hamlet to the south-east of Hobart, 40 people survived by walking into the sea and standing around a small boat in which pregnant women and small children sat. The fires even burnt the seaweed on the beach at the waters' edge. Thousands of sheep cattle and other livestock were burnt alive on farms in southern Tasmania. At least 1400 buildings were incinerated, 1500 cars destroyed and 62 Tasmanians lost their lives.

Communications went down and as I sat impotently in Melbourne trying to find out if my parents and aunts houses had survived – they were in bush surroundings in the foothills of Mount Nelson in the harbourside suburb at Sandy Bay. My brothers Nick and Philip manage to help save several houses in their neighbourhood, in company with their friends. The Bowdens were lucky but many of their neighbours lost everything.

Having established at last that all my family was safe I continued on my way to Singapore to reclaim my car (which Ros had been happily using) and getting back to work. A month later my boss Peter Hollinshead it called me into his office and said that it been decided to send me to the

ABC's North American office in New York. I said that I didn't want to go, thank you very much.

Peter said that it wasn't for me to say. My former colleague in Tasmania, David Wilson (who was be acting in my old job as Supervisor of Talks), was one of the unfortunate victims of the fire. He and his wife and young children were homeless, having lost absolutely all they possessed. The ABC's new general manager Talbot Duckmanton, decided that he would help them with their immediate accommodation problem by giving them an overseas posting. New York was been suggested, but the ABC Representative there, Charles Buttrose, was horrified when he heard that David Wilson was not a trained journalist. He argued that the office was too small to support a Talks man who was not able to file news stories. So it was decided David would go to Singapore – a bigger office – and I would go to New York.

I was a reluctant starter. Ros and I were very happy together and moving on would be sweet goodbye to her and also my flat just off Orchard Road, servant, and new car in a region I found endlessly fascinating. Somehow, I wasn't ready to propose to Ros and in those days the ABC didn't allow non-married partners to accompany their correspondents. Even if Ros had said yes to the unasked question we would've had to get married in a scrambling rush. So I gallantly said, 'Cheerio it's been great', and shot through. Ros told me later that she was surprised by this but got on with her life by signing up with Gleneagles hospital for a two-year contract.

David Wilson (one of the most boring people who ever lived) and his wife Annette arrived in Singapore in time for a week's handover. I arrived at their hotel with my car and said, well here we are in one of the world's great shopping bazaars. I'm at your disposal where would you like to go? Annette said, 'Could you take me somewhere where we can buy some plastic coat-hangers'?

Peter Hollinshead was putting a brave face on things. He was a quick and shrewd judge of people and he could see David was going to be a challenge. Hollings didn't like mollycoddling people. He liked self-starters who just got on with things. There wasn't much I could show or tell David. He knew about tape recorders and editing. The rest was up to him.

I had to unload my car at the last minute. I sold my beloved Brabham Viva to a beaming Chinese who (a) knew it was practically a brand-new car and (b) I had to sell it. I wasn't in a good bargaining position and lost heaps. Events moved so quickly that was hardly time even for an office farewell, although a brief drinks and nibbles were arranged. I was quite glum about leaving although I suppose I should've been relishing new challenges. New York seemed a poor swap for my beloved Singapore.

Charles Buttrose, the ABC's North American representative, was kind enough to meet me at John F Kennedy airport with Peter Barnett who was in town from the Washington office. Peter told me later that as they saw me walking towards them, Charles thought I was wearing suede shoes. (I wasn't). ABC News men thought Talks people wore suede shoes, had long hair and were of doubtful sexuality.) He said, to Peter, 'Christ I hope they haven't sent me one of those Talks poofters'.

We drove by taxi into the concrete canyons in New York where the ABC had a suite of offices in the Rockefeller Centre on Sixth Avenue (Avenue of the Americas) while the other ABC – the American Broadcasting Company – had a skyscraper just up the road. This confusion between the two was to cause me considerable anguish seven months later in my New York term.

Charles Moses was the ABC's longest serving General Managers, who held that job for 30 years! Charles Buttrose was Moses' D Pub & Con – Director of Publicity and Concerts in ABC jargon. He was an ex-newspaper executive, having worked for two notoriously cantankerous press barons – Ezra Norton on the *Daily Mirror* and Frank Packer on the *Daily Telegraph*. As D Pub and Con he had not only been in charge of all the ABCs publicity and promotions in radio and television, he was also the supremo of the ABC's huge concert empire, which had symphony orchestras in each Australian State and co-ordinated and looked after a stellar cast of eminent conductors and soloists who toured Australia for the ABC. It was an area close to the heart of the former general manager so Charles

Moses, who loved entertaining the overseas conductors, violinists and pianists – many of whom only toured Australia because they liked his style. Buttrose, who had been also being a singer in his varied career, knew a lot about the classical music business and welcomed a good party or two along the way.

Parties and bonhommie were not the forte, however, of the incoming General Manager Talbot Duckmanton, who not only distanced himself from this kind of personal relationships with overseas artists, but was quick to move on Moses' inner circle and put in his own team. Which was why Buttrose was exiled to New York. Once the initial disappointment of his loss of power and influence subsided, he recovered his customary ebullience and begin to build up the North American office. He and his wife Margot loved New York and he quickly established a rapport with legendary musical entrepreneurs like Sol Hurok as well as with soloists and conductors. Being an old journo he found it difficult to stop acting like a news editor to the ABC correspondents in North America who certainly weren't responsible to him editorially – but to their Sydney masters. I must say I always found Charlie's suggestions worthwhile and I often took them up. If I didn't he wasn't fussed.

Peter Barnett had just left New York to open the ABCs Washington Bureau and Terry Brown, an ABC News journalist from Sydney, had replaced him. Peter had suggested I take over the lease of his studio apartment in New York which was splendidly situated on Central Park South near Columbus Circle, with a fabulous view right up the full length of Central Park. I was within walking distance of Carnegie Hall and the Lincoln Centre. It was also close enough to the Rockefeller Centre for me to be able to walk to work. (There was a lot of development going on at the time and I remember seeing fine flakes of asbestos floating down on the Sixth Avenue like snow from the new skyscrapers under construction). The apartment only had one room, a small kitchen and bathroom, but that was fine by me. The sofa pulled out into a king size bed that was extreme comfortable. I also inherited 'Dear old Miss Etta', Peter's black cleaning lady who was later to rob me before I left New York.

By November I had adjusted to New York on the practical and professional level but emotionally was a bit of a basket case. I was lonely and I missed Ros, but I wasn't admitting that to myself. They had been no contact between us for seven months. A weekend away changed all that. My fellow colleague as former cadet reporter on the *Mercury* in Hobart, Michael Philip, had stopped adventuring on yachts in central America, and married an American girl before changing course and becoming a university lecturer in English at the University of Maryland in Annapolis. Mike and Susie invited me down to spend a few days with them. I left New York with one of the worst hangovers I have ever had, and I resorted to my emergency green pills. These were prescribed to me by an obliging chemist friend in Launceston for unspeakable hangovers. I'm not sure what they were – probably amphetamines. I only had a few left but I took two of them as I boarded the train to Annapolis. They were magic. Cool streams of water flowed through my numbed brain. I sat in the carriage looking out the window at the bleak winter landscape and admitted to myself that I missed Ros like hell and had been a bloody fool leaving her in Singapore. At the end of the journey I was still thinking about her and resolved to do something about the absurd situation I had got myself into when I got back to New York.

Mike and Susie had just produced their first son, Tas. Always a boating enthusiasts Mike had built a traditional wooden cat boat and we sailed it to sheltered anchorages in Chesapeake Bay and picnicked, while Susie breastfed Tas. Their obvious commitment and happiness fuelled my determination to try to reunite with Ros. I had turned 30 in August and wandered miserably around Times Square in New York on my birthday wondering what I was doing with my life. I think many young people get a strong nesting urge at that time in their lives, but before I took the green pills, I had thought marriage was not for me.

When I got back to New York I still felt strongly that I should contact Ros. It was highly likely, I thought, she would tell me to get stuffed. She might even have another fella. I knew my international times when I put my phone call through to the nursing quarters at Gleneagles Hospital in

Singapore around nine in the morning to catch Ros before she went to work. What I couldn't know it was that she had just gone to sleep after finishing a week's nightshift. The Cantonese hospital switchboard operator misheard heard America. She told a groggy Ros that Tim Bowden was calling from Malacca in nearby Malaya.

I had my spiel all worked out, but it was a difficult and call for both of us. It started awkwardly. Ros asked me first what I was doing in Malacca. We sorted that out and I blurted out words to the effect that I've been missing her like hell and I was a bloody fool to leave her in Singapore and how about we got married. There was a long silence. Then she said, 'Tim that's not fair'.

It was not the answer I expected, but it wasn't a dead-set 'no'. We agreed that Ros could not really respond to one telephone call out of the blue after seven months silence, and that we should write to each other and keep talking on the phone. (I still have Ros's letters). She had been deeply hurt by my sudden and cavalier departure but had she thought she had got over me. We did agree that it would've been difficult to get spliced when I was posted so suddenly to New York, so perhaps it was better to explore possibilities as she suggested. We kept talking and writing for two weeks. Ros still hadn't said yes. Then there was utter silence for ten days.

I moped around the office and was grumpy. In Singapore Ros – who had actually sent a telegram giving the green light to our future together – wondered why I hadn't responded. Perhaps I had changed my mind. She had sent telegram to me, care of the ABC Avenue of the Americas, New York. It arrived at the skyscraper inhabited by the American Broadcasting Company just up the road, and was eventually returned to sender. I got back from lunch one day to find the office manager, Lydia Hatcher had typed out a short phonogram from Ros and popped it in my typewriter.

It was in a kind of code. In Singapore and Malaya the expression 'lah' is used as an emphasis word. Ros's message simply said 'Can Lah!' and also wished me a merry Christmas.

I couldn't contain my joy and confessed to Lydia (who had guessed the truth anyway despite the Malay code). The ABC crew I worked with had

We both had relatives in England, so that is where we actually tied the knot, in a small Anglican Church on the Backs at Cambridge. That was now I had to hire a formal Morning Suit (the only time I ever wore one in my life) because in those days you had to be married in a church.

been finding me difficult to live with. New York suddenly seemed a sunny and brighter place even with winter approaching.

Long distance negotiations continued, but in a more buoyant mood. The complications of getting together again were awesome. We agreed that it would be best to get married in England. Ros had cousins in Devon and I had relatives in Cambridge where my Uncle Philip was a Don at Caius College, and he was also a Fellow of the Royal Society. He and his wife Margot Bowden were kind enough to offer us their home, *Finella,* for a wedding reception on the Backs at Cambridge. Ros's cousin Dick Spurway would give her away. My first Singapore flat-mate, Bob Hart, now working for Reuters Newsagency in London, would be my best man. (As coincidence would have it I had been able to provide the same service for him a couple of weeks earlier.) The bad news was that Ros could not be released from her two-year hospital contract for three months. We set the date for 20 April 1968. In order to conform with British laws (and to have the banns read in church for three consecutive weeks) I had to be resident in Britain for a month. I had some holidays owing, and the ABC obligingly arranged for me to be transferred to the London Office for two weeks, although I had to pay my own return airfares to England. It was not possible to get married under a tree in those days – always a risky prospect in England with its weather – and since neither of us was keen on a registry office job, a church wedding it had to be.

Ros arrived in London a week before the wedding. Our meeting was curiously formal. In the way it represented the awkwardness of our strange intra-country courtship. Both of us, as we admitted to each other much later, were wondering if we have done the right thing after all. I remember taking Ros to a pub for a drink. We sat at a table talking about the arrangements for the wedding. There were occasional silences. After one of these, I suddenly said to her, 'How are your teeth'?

Ros cracked up. 'What on earth do you mean'? I explained that we were in the land of a beneficial National Health scheme that encompassed free dentistry. She said her teeth were just fine thanks and giggled again.

We were married on 20 April 1968 in a little High Anglican church, St Peters on a hill near the Backs at Cambridge. My cousin Piers arranged for a friend to take in and play a tiny harpsichord. The rather austere clergyman must have been surprised at the smell of brandy on the bride's breath. It was 11 am, and her cousin Dick Spurway said they needed some fortification on their way to church. Ros was in full white bridal splendour and my best man Bob Hart and I dressed up in hired formal morning suits, with cutaway coats and top hats. Our wedding photographs caused most Australians to burst out laughing.

Sadly my uncle Philip Bowden could not attend the reception. He had just been operated on for the lung cancer that was to kill him five months later. Thinking back, we shouldn't really have gone ahead with the reception at *Finella* under the circumstances, but Margot would not hear of us cancelling.

I mucked up the train bookings and Ros and I had to leave a bloody good party for a slow train to London in time for us to catch a plane to Spain the following morning. We decided to honeymoon in the island of Ibiza, in the Balearic Islands in the Mediteranean.

I wanted Ros to see a bullfight – I was thinking of the ambience of Hemingway's classic book, *Death in the Afternoon*. Ibiza did not have a full-scale bull ring but some of the local lads turned on a demonstration for the tourists with some young bulls, twirling their capes and stepping nimbly away from the bulls, which did have well-developed horns. It was all rather second rate and some of the audience jeered. The Spanish boys then invited anyone from the audience to come and do better.

I remarked to my wife of two days that I wouldn't be so silly. Ros said, 'But they are only very little bulls'. (She later denied ever having said that.) 'Oh', I said, and unwisely vaulted into the ring and grabbed a red cape from one of the Spanish lads. A bull charged towards me and I waved the red cape at it. It took no notice and butted me straight in the chest, fortunately with its head and not its horns. I hit the ground, but managed to scramble out of the ring before I was further trampled, to the laughter of both the tourists and the Spanish would-be toreadors.

We took a ferry to Barcelona, hired a car and drove to Toledo. We wanted to see the townscape made famous by the artist El Greco. Ros became obsessed with mediaeval churches. I don't mind one or two, but she was indefatigable. 'What's that' she asked, pointing to some carved wooden panels. Sometimes if you say something quickly and confidently enough you can get away with it. 'Seven Stations of the Cross', I said a little too glibly. Apparently there are more. Ros was onto me, and 'Seven Stations of the Cross' became a metaphor for spouse engendered bullshit in the years ahead.

Once we returned to New York, we found Peter Barnett's bachelor apartment I had inherited, with its panoramic view of Central Park, was too cramped for us, and we begin to negotiate for a bigger apartment at the back of the building. After the airfares, the expense of the wedding, and our honeymoon we were flat broke and I suggested that Ros get a job while I went happily back to my routine of being a foreign correspondent. It was a fairly rugged introduction to New York for her. She found a job as a nurse, with an elderly New York plastic surgeon, Dr Aufrich. His speciality was doing nose jobs for young Jewish girls. Although he was in his late 70s, Aufrich could plough through four or five operations in a morning. It was a fairly brutal business, leaving patients looking as though they're done around or two with Mohammed Ali (or Cassius Clay as he then was). Aufrich had a set style, which was known as 'The Aufrich nose'. Ros' nose was much admired by the mothers of incoming patients and wanted to know if it had been done by her boss!

Because of the time difference with Australia, I did not start at the ABC office till 10 am and the pace did not pick up until early afternoon. I would be asleep and snoring when Ros took herself off at 6 am to Dr Aufrich's nose factory. Sometimes I would have a game of squash with my boss Charlie Buttrose (who was a fit man in his late 50s) and Terry Brown, the News journalist, before a leisurely lunch. Ros would stagger into the apartment in the late afternoon and try to think about what she might cook for dinner. (She found Peggy Bracken's *I Hate to Cook* book an inspiration for a quick culinary fixes) but sometimes I would ring and say I was going to have a few drinks at the United Nations and I'd be late. It's a wonder she stayed with me. Ros didn't like New York much. She found the legendary New York rudeness to be certainly without charm and simply unpleasant, after the warm friendliness of Chinese Singapore. She said later the year in New York with me turned her into a feminist and later having teenage sons forced her to be a fascist!

We were both grateful for the presence in New York of Geoff and Rachel Miller. They had an apartment on the East Side that we used to go there for dinner on weekend excursions. Family life in a New York apartment was a challenge. They had to rig up swings in their apartment doorways for their two lively little boys because it wasn't safe for them to play unsupervised in the local park.

Geoff was the First Secretary of the Australian Mission to the United Nations and I used to have long conversations with him about Australian foreign policy. I recall he once mused that, 'If we accepted that Australia was profoundly threatened by Communist nations to our north, and that if the teetering domino 'democracies' like South Vietnam fell and the Communists poured south to invade our big empty country – well then then, our foreign policy with its support for the Vietnam War made good sense. But on the other hand if…' his voice trailed off and we both stared into our drinks without speaking.

It was Geoff who came up with the Gravity Theory of Communism that was linked to Mercator's Projection – adding to the paranoia of Australia's fiercely anti-Communist foreign policy. 'Consider', he said during one of these discussions,' if the view of the world most often featured on maps didn't have China and the densely populated countries in Southeast Asia poised over a big empty Australia'. We decided (over a few excellent Australian white wines), that it was our position at the bottom of the map that gave the impression that the Asian hordes would seep down – like sand into an empty glass – and fill us up.

During one leisurely Sunday when we needed some beer, I said to Geoff that I'd go and get some. He said to use his car, a somewhat battered Chev Corvette. It was of course, graced with diplomatic numberplates.

On my way downtown to a corner liquor store, another driver cut in on my lane and I had to brake suddenly. Without thinking I gave him 'the finger'. To my chagrin and some anxiety, he drew alongside me at the next traffic lights. People can get shot by road rage maddened lunatics for doing things like that in New York. The driver motioned me to wind down my window. He leaned across and said, 'That wasn't very diplomatic'!

We were fortunate to be living very close to the Lincoln Centre so when we heard Joan Sutherland was to appear in *La Sonnambula* we manage to get tickets. It was an electrifying performance particularly when the sleepwalking Joan walked across the narrow suspended plank which bent alarmingly under her not inconsiderable weight. We were sitting behind a middle-aged gay couple – opera buffs – who had front row balcony seats. At the first intermission they recognised our Australian accents and thanked us effusively for Joan! We said we were very pleased about her too. They both stood up and insisted we take their front row seats for the rest of the performance. New York could be like that.

Early in the morning of 5 June 1968 Ros and I were sound asleep (after coming in later of a dinner party ends bracket and the phone rang. It was Terry Hughes, an Australian freelance who worked from our ABC Office in New York. 'Bobby Kennedy's been assassinated', he said.

'You're joking!'

'Switch on your television then'. I did in time to see the chaos in the kitchen of the Ambassador Hotel in Los Angeles shortly after Sirhan Sirhan had shot the Democratic presidential candidate as he was leaving a dinner.

I rang Terry Brown, dragged on some clothes and ran through dark and deserted New York streets to the office. Both of us were battling to get our minds into gear in our early morning stupor. It was coming up to evening news time in Australia. We only had minutes to put something together. Using our brand-new studio we grabbed some sound actuality from CBS and tried to summarise what we been able to glean from television and radio sources in the time available to us. We rang Sydney and got ready to deliver a package. Terry and I began our 'Mutt and Jeff' routine, but fluffed badly. I shouted down the phone to Sydney, 'Bugger it! Stop the bloody tape and we'll do it again'. I thought we were talking to technicians in the Sydney newsroom recording our efforts to broadcast later. The thought of television did not occur to me for a moment, nor did it cross the minds of anyone in Sydney to tell me. Unbeknown to us we had been fed live to ABC TV for the 7 pm National News. I'm told the announcer James Dibble smiled gently and remarked that, 'The boys in New York seem to be under some pressure'! Fortunately our second effort went off without more profanity. I didn't hear about my Coast to Coast gaffe until days later. I could well have used stronger language. It was entirely unprofessional not to tell us we were patched into a live television news bulletin.

Bobby Kennedy's assassination was devastating to a nation still finding it hard to come to grips with his brother Jack's killing. Black Americans knew it was bad news for them. Martin Luther King had been assassinated in April and there was widespread rioting in the ghettos. Opposition to the Vietnam war was also ripping the nation apart and had destroyed Lyndon Baines Johnson who had announced on 31 March that he would not stand again for the Presidency. I had missed both of these big stories because I was absent on leave getting married. But I was on hand to help report the anointing of Richard Nixon to be Republican candidate for the presidency in Miami in August and his Vice Presidential running mate Spiro Agnew. Spiro who? everyone asked at the time.

Ros and I moved into the two bedroom apartment we'd negotiated at the rear of the same apartment block on Central Park South, losing our spectacular view but able to entertain visiting friends. Robyn Nevin and Barry Crook came to New York with their daughter Emily then only six weeks old. The travel had upset the young baby and no one got much sleep. Evil Nurse Ros Geddes came to the rescue and convinced the doubtful Robyn that Emily had to have a dummy – not only that with honey on it! We all slept blissfully.

Gay pride was blossoming in New York and Terry Hughes took us to a gay nightclub. I found it an extraordinary experience. They didn't seem to mind straight couples being there and there was a degree of eroticism on the dance floor that Ros and I found exhilarating. Robyn stayed at home as she was looking after Emily. Big Barry did demur when I asked him for a dance but relented. The only difficulty we had was working out who would lead.

On Thanksgiving eve we got together with some Australian friends and drank a lethal champagne punch with strawberries floating in it. We woke up the next day with atrocious hangovers, jolted from sleep by the sound of a brass band. Our apartment was on the seventh floor and I looked out the window towards Seventh Avenue to see a giant Snoopy, followed by an even bigger dinosaur at eye level. I honestly thought I had delerium tremens and called to Ros to make sure she could see them too. They were huge gas-filled, tethered balloons, which were part of the annual Macy's Thanksgiving Day parade.

By 1969 Talbot Duckmanton had been General Manager of the ABC for four years – with another thirteen to go. His taste for overseas travel was already well-developed. I think he thought of himself as a kind of foreign minister, with the ABC offices abroad as his embassies. He was not the kind of general manager who had much to do with his troops – that is in Australia. But on overseas trips he had a personality change and became outgoing and remarkably even gregarious up to a point.

In the comforting ambience of the overseas posts he had time to get to know his ambassadors. Although Charles Buttrose, the died-in-the-wool Moses man had been exiled to New York, constant visits there convinced Duckmanton that he should be bought back to a senior job in Sydney. But that was not until 1970. Peter Hollinshead in Singapore had got the nod first, and rang me in March 1968 to say Duckmanton has appointed him Head of Current Affairs in both radio and television. Peter said he wanted me to return to Sydney to be responsible for starting up the evening radio current affairs programme *PM* to complement the morning's *AM* which had started in 1967.

Ros was delighted, as her ambivalence about New York never really diminished. She knew Sydney very well, although I had never lived there. We started making plans for our return. The Millers had made us clucky and we started to talk children. When it was announced that we were leaving, our cleaner Miss Etta used her last visit to relieve us of a portable radio, Ros's prized antique saphire brooch and fur coat. We were stupid enough not to pack small items ourselves and the New York movers added to the tally by helping themselves to a rose-tinted jade Buddha that Ros gad given to me as a wedding present, various silver knick-knacks and various other little treasures we didn't miss until months later.

As our departure from New York moved closer, I found myself walking along 59th Street at the rear of our apartment block – a narrow one-way lane – I saw a motorist about to reverse back into a parking spot he was lucky to see. A taxi, which could have held back until he got in, roared right up behind him and the driver started blaring his horn. The man just trying to park had no choice but to abandon his precious parking space and was forced drive off around the block again. I raced up to the taxi drivers' open window and shouted at him that he was an 'Inconsiderate mother fucker why did you have to bully some poor bastard he was only trying to park. Bloody typical of you New York taxi drivers', I heard myself shouting, 'Why don't you wake up to yourself you miserable prick?' He put his head out the window and replied in kind. I think we both felt better. I took the elevator up to our apartment and told Ros I thought I'd been in New York too long.

. . . .

Roz and I were extremely happy to be back in Sydney and enjoyed life in the Kirribilli flat. We started to talk about having kids and tore down all the contraceptive barriers – with no immediate results. I might have had the impressive title of executive producer of the new current affairs radio program *PM* , but that carried a salary of only $6000 a year, which wasn't much even in 1969. We are agonised how we could afford a house. From New York we had seen in the *Sydney Morning Herald* that Mosman houses were selling for $16,000 – how on earth were we going to afford that kind of money? By the time we got home the prices had shot up to the high twenties! We decided to start saving for a deposit, and bought in some economics. Home-brewed beer was one of them. It was before the days of home brewing shops with sealed fermenters for fancy recipes. It was also illegal to brew beer above 2 per cent alcohol, although I figured if my hand shook bit as the sugar went in, the home brewing beer police would perhaps give me the benefit of the doubt. We brewed in an open plastic bucket. The result was barely drinkable but it was cheap. We drank most of it ourselves – our guests politely declining. The open bucket brewing was letting in bugs that gave it a slight taste of cider. It was a perfect demonstration of my father's deeply held belief that, 'Home-brewed beer is like farting – your own seems alright'!

We shared a half cabin motorboat on Middle Harbour with fellow expatriate Tasmanian Brian King (who was in Sydney as a reporter with television's *Four Corners*), swam on the outer harbour beaches and had picnics. Ros did not miss New York. She was, however, surprised at how backward attitudes were in Australia towards women. Ros' interest in the growing feminist movement was not only triggered by being in New York married to me, but by very quaint rules and regulations still restricting what women could and couldn't do in Australia. Take hotels for instance. Women were not allowed in public bars – apart from the barmaids that worked there. Women could only be served in the ladies lounges. We had just spent time in London and New York where such absurd rules and regulations were unknown.

Not long after we arrived in Sydney in 1968, Ros and I decided to see a movie in the city. It was a hot summers night, we were early and felt like a drink. Knowing Sydney's strange drinking habits I didn't want any trouble. Surely a hotel of international standing would be safe enough? We walked into the Wentworth and headed for the cocktail bar. Unfortunately I could not go in with Ros because I was not wearing a tie. Where could we drink together then? 'Alas sir, the public bar doesn't serve women and we have no other area where you can be served'. This got Ros' dander up and she shot the messenger with great vigour. (Sydney was even hosting an international tourism convention at the time!)

We walked up the street, still thirsty and I saw a tavern on George Street and headed up the stairs looking for the Ladies Lounge but there wasn't one. The publican spotted us and trotted down the stairs very agitated and said Ros could not have a drink on the premises. I said, 'Well I suppose you won't mind if I do', and walked into the public bar, ordered a schooner of VB and went back to where Ros was waiting at the bottom of the stairs and handed it to her so we could share it. The publican and was suspicious and had stayed in the background. He came charging down the stairs and tried to grab the glass from Ros' hand. With some skill she directed the entire ice-cold contents of the schooner into his crotch. Had she not been a woman he would have punched her. I thought it wise that we left fairly quickly before he had a go at me – but we still didn't get a drink before seeing a movie.

By 1969 We had moved from our rented flat in Kirribili and started paying off a house in Northbridge on the Lower North Shore. (By then I started the evening current affairs program *PM* as its Executive Producer, but only for a year when Peter Hollinshead wanted me to join *This Day* Tonight as an Assistant Producer although I knew sod-all about television. Ros still wasn't pregnant and we got a dog as a child substitute. We got him from the public pound as a puppy, hoping he wouldn't grow too large. We should have looked more carefully at his feet. He was a cross between some sort of hound and – well no one ever really knew. Spike was a singular dog and soon worked out when he heard the closing theme *This Day Tonight*, Ros would let him ride in the car when she came to pick me up from the ABC's television studios in Artarmon. As soon as he heard the music, he would rush to the screen and howl with joy. I think we manage to get this performance on video and re-played on the program.

We started having tests to see why Ros wasn't conceiving. Mine was straightforward enough, although I remember getting a bit bored with it all. Sperm samples had to be got in for testing within an hour. We ran short of containers and my last effort was delivered – with a raised eyebrow by the female technician who received it – in a Chinese sweet and sour pickle bottle.

It would have been better if we had gone immediately to a fertility specialist. Instead, the gynaecologist she attended had a pet theory that redheads were uptight. Ros wasn't. She was a most relaxed and calm person

– well most of the time. So he prescribed a sedative, but as she wasn't uptight anyway, this treatment was ludicrous and we got sick of all this and decided to adopt.

As a final check we did visit a fertility specialist – expecting him to confirm infertility. He explained the three basic test for this, enough wrigglers in my ejaculation, confirming that Ros was ovulating, and the density of mucus in the tubes leading to her ovaries. The first two were okay, so what about the third? While I was standing by, he busied himself with two glass rods, and stepped back from a reclining Ros, stretching a strain of mucus between them. 'Look', he said triumphantly. 'No self-respecting sperm could swim through that'! The pompous ass who provided the sedative had not even bothered to test those basic three essential links in elementary fertility trilogy. I'd like to name him, but he may not be dead.

I mentioned that we were planning to adopt. 'Why', said our fertility specialist? 'You don't get rid of your car just because it needs a new carburettor'. Prescribing some pills for Ros, he said if there were too many in the bottle she could 'Use them to fertilise dahlias, and you'll have some prize-winning blooms'.

We were rather attracted to the idea of adoption so anyway decided to go ahead. Social attitudes to unmarried mothers were about to change when the new Whitlam Labor government would make single-parent benefits more available, but in 1971 it was still possible to adopt babies within Australia with only a relatively short waiting time. We didn't even need to consider the possibility of an inter-country adoption – which we would have, of course, if babies have been unavailable locally. A social worker came to interview us and we settled down to wait, not knowing how lucky we were.

On the personal front, things were much brighter. Early in September the Bowden's had a welcome phone call. After a wait – appropriately enough – of nine months, we were told that a baby boy was awaiting collection at Crown Street hospital. Barnaby John Bowden was only nine days old, small but perfectly formed at a modest five pounds – and not much longer than the wine bottle against which he was photographed soon after we got him home. Only Spike the dog looked crestfallen. He seemed to know he would no longer be top dog in the family hierarchy and he was right.

By this time I was working with *This Day Tonight* and the ABC Television Studios were conveniently only about ten minutes drive from our Northbridge house.

One of the producers, Ken Chown, arranged for a bulk bottling of red wine for those at *This Day Tonight* who wanted to take advantage of it. There was considerable interest and I offered our house for this pleasant exercise. Three huge wooden casks were unloaded in our carport, plastic tubing insert and umpteen dozen washed bottles were filled and corked. Not all the wine went into the bottles but it was a good day. As not everyone was able to take the bottles with them at the end of the day, our dining room had some 30 cartons of freshly decanted red stacked against its walls.

At Northbridge I carved out a barbecue from a solid sandstone ledge near our backdoor – nearly losing my toes in the sudden rockfall – and life was good. Our application for another adoption could not be satisfied for a statutory two years. In fact, it took nearly three years before we got Guy Philip Bowden because social attitudes to adoption were changing so rapidly. The Whitlam Labour government introduced a single mothers' allowance, and the burgeoning women's movement certainly believed that it to believe that it was better for the mother and child to stay together, so very few Australian babies were available.

One day I had a call from Michael Symons, a producer with the ABC's Science Unit, asking if Ros and I, as adoptive parents, would take part in a debate on adoption. The main issue at the time was whether adopted children should be allowed, or indeed encouraged, to locate their birth mothers after they reach the age of 18. Michael asked what my attitude was. I hadn't given the question much and said I was against it. Michael seemed pleased and signed this us both up for the live radio debate. On the way into the studio Ros asked me what the issues were. I told her what I had said. 'But that's not what I think at all', she said. 'Adopted children should be encouraged to find their birth parents. I think that is terribly important'!

Michael Symons met us at the door. Being a producer myself I was embarrassed about what I had to say. 'Michael, there is good news and bad news. Ros doesn't agree with me and thinks adopted children should be able to find their birth mothers. But I'm hard-line'. He looked relieved. The fulcrum for the debate was an adopted Scottish woman who had, against the odds, manage to find her birth mother in South Africa through a new organisation called Adoption Triangle, which facilitated such meetings. It had been an emotional and cathartic experience which she ultimately found rewarding and she had gained a large extended family. However, there were stories of attempted reunions which did not have good out-comes. Some birth mothers were in new relationships and felt they could not tell their partners about having had a child, and reject any contact completely. Such a rejection could be devastating to the adopted person. My spinal-cord reaction as an adopted parent was to feel threatened by the possibility of a birthmother entering the picture. The Scottish woman eyed me off with some distaste. As the debate proceeded I realised I was talking absolute crap. Because of my promise to Michael I tried to maintain my advertised point of view, but I had really changed my views as the discussion went on and they stayed changed.

The real drama concerned with this debate had already happened within the Science Unit. Michael Symons wanted to find a young adopted adult, prepared to talk about the issue from his or her perspective on air. One of the Science Unit support staff thought she might be able to help – she had a nephew then in his early 20s who had been adopted, and she would sound him out. She telephoned her nephew, explained about the adoption debate and asked him if he would come on the program to talk about his own adoption. There was rather a long pause – and he said that, if she didn't mind, he need to think a bit more about it before deciding. 'You see, before your telephone call I didn't know I was adopted...'

Ros agreed with me that it wasn't my finest hour.

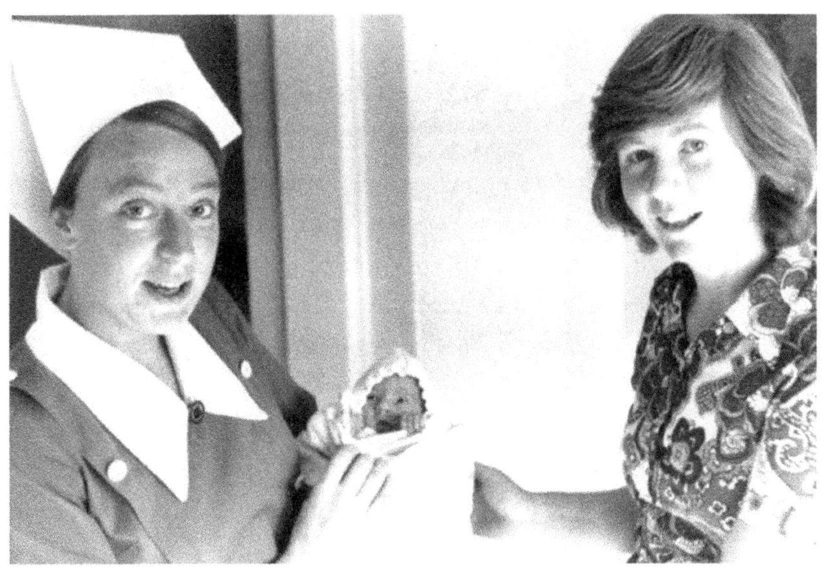

Hand-over of our first adopted boy Barnaby to Ros outside Sydney's Crown Street Hospital.

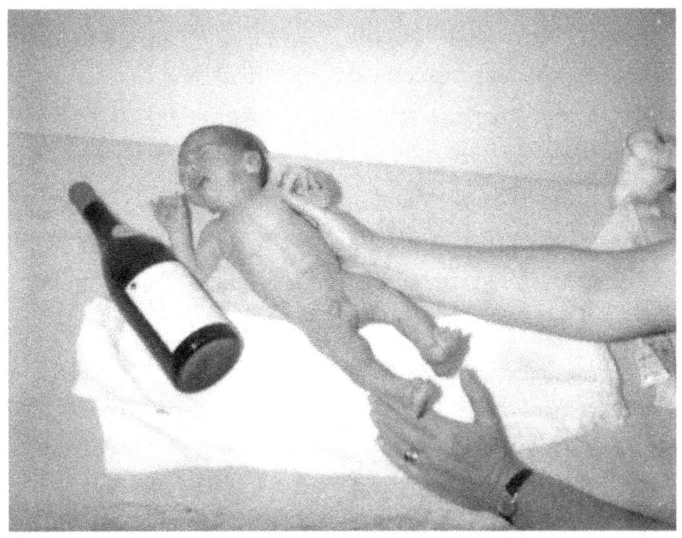

Nine days old Barnaby measured against wine bottle.

3

'Hello to Barnaby and Guy'

By early 1974 I was becoming increasingly frustrated with my situation with Radio Current Affairs. The previous year I had been working as one of two daily Producers for the ABC TV's flagship current affairs program *This Day Tonight* which had reverted to the control of the powerful (and rather unforgiving) management of one Ken Watts, the ABC's Controller of Television, who had started *TDT* in 1987, and had moved his original management team back in control, and I was as popular with the New Order as a poisonous snake in a lucky dip. I had been returned to Current Affairs Radio now run by a most unpleasant character, Russell Warner, who delighted in making my role in his fiefdom as humiliating as he could. He was very good at that. I felt it was time for a change.

Fortunately I had been at the ABC long enough to qualify for three months long service leave on full pay. There was also an option of taking six months leave on half pay. If I added in in my holidays for the following year we could make it seven months. There are only so many windows in your life when you can take an extended break like that. Most people travelled before they married and settled down, then to have to wait until their children are grown up and they retire. Our boy Barnaby was only 18 months old, so schooling didn't have to be considered. Ros had been doing some part time journalism – writing happy migrant stories for the Department of Immigration – and we had even been able to pay back my Uncle Max the $4000 he lent us to help buy our house in Sydney's North Shore suburb Northbridge. (Later Ros started doing freelance interviews for the ABC, despite my helpful advice that she didn't have a good voice for radio. She soon proved me wrong and in view of what we were about to attempt, that was just as well.)

We decided we would buy a second-hand Volkswagen Kombi and head north in June up the east coast to Cairns, across to Normanton and

Cloncurry, on to the Berkeley Tablelands to Tennant Creek and up to Darwin. Then we would consider how we would get back. Tasmania seemed a good place to spend Christmas, and after that we would face up to whatever professional future beckoned in the ABC – if there was one.

I broached the possibility of an attachment with Radio Drama and Features with its Director Dick Connolly and his deputy Julie-Anne Ford. They had no positions vacant at the time, but things might be different in seven-months time. They were keen however to have me on board, which was a welcome change.

We followed up an advertisement for a 1967 split-screen Kombi which had been converted, by its owner, into a camper. It had a small gas and electric fridge just inside the van door, and a table and bench seats which converted into a double bed. The rear compartment over the engine would be a bedroom for Barnaby. For reasons I can't remember we called the Kombi Gertrude, shortened to Gertie. The Italian guy who sold it to us nearly cried when we drove off. Kombi's do that to people. I never met anyone who drove one who is not a splendid human being.

To carry our gear we found a 6 x 4 trailer and I installed a full-length roof rack on Gertie's top to carry a big marquee tent, and chairs and tables to put up if you came across a nice place where we might stay for a week. I installed a wooden bench and storage bins across the back of the trailer as travelling kitchen, and a 60-litre water tank with a pump attached. There was still plenty of room for an axe and spade – essential for bush camping – stocks of tinned food and other gear. I also fitted an awning above the side door so we could have shade when we stopped. How on earth I expected Gertie's tiny 1500 cc engine to pull all this around Australia was another unanswered rhetorical question. A baby seat for Barnaby fitted in snuggly between the two front seats and we decorated his sleeping area over the rear-mounted engine with kiddy transfers.

By the time we equipped ourselves with all this gear we had less than $1000 to last us for the next seven months. Even at 1974 values, that wasn't going to be enough. We hoped to support our travel by Ros' free-lancing for ABC Radio. I was not able to work as I was on staff and taking my long service leave. If Ros could not sell her interviews, we would have to come back with our tails between their legs.

A German mechanic in North Sydney, Karl, checked out Gerties' engine. I asked him about having a temperature gauge fitted. 'Vat for', shouted Carl. 'Do you vant to get ulcers'? He was right. It's a wonder that little air-cooled engine didn't melt, considering the load we were carrying and pulling. But it just went on chuntering along with that distinctive Volkswagen sound.

We rented our Northridge house to a current affairs colleague, Hillary Roots, and prepared to head off on our odyssey. Ros' parents lived at Mount Colah, on Sydney's northern fringe, and we pulled in to spend our last night in Sydney with them. Their driveway fronted onto a rather steep hill. The following morning, after our farewells, I revved the motor and engaged first gear. To my horror, Gertie – loaded trailer and full roof rack – ground to a halt before we got to the top of the hill. If we couldn't get out of Ros' parents drive on day one how the hell were we to get around Australia? It was tricky backing the trailer back into the driveway but I managed it. With even more revs I engaged the clutch and tried again. It happened again. I realised we couldn't get a decent run on the hill from the driveway. Sweating and cursing I manage to back the trailer right down to the bottom of the hill – which anyone who has tried to back cranky trailers with a short wheelbase would know is no easy task.

At least we could get a run on the hill and with enormous relief, Gertie just made it over the top on the third go – but I had to slip the clutch a bit at the last moment. 'At least most of outback Australia is flat', I said to Ros.

I can still remember the wonderful surge of exhilaration, freedom and excitement of embarking on that adventure. The sun was shining, one of Barnaby's favourite tapes was playing on the cassette player to his great delight, and the whole of Australia was waiting for us – well half of it anyway.

. . . .

We were in no hurry to get to Queensland, as Ros would have to earn our keep with radio interviews with colourful characters adding to our modest expenses pot of $1000 which was not going to last us for long enough. We found the ABC's Rural Department, with its plethora of local magazine programs, was the best bet.

So as we moved north through NSW we took byways down to the coast and pitched camp in some terrific locations, where we took our marquee tent off the roof rack, camping chairs and beds, and were very comfortable indeed. Ros needed the Kombi of course to do her interviews, and I minded Barnaby. When she came back with her items, I transferred her items to quarter-inch tape, and edited them on a splicing block and a razor blade, typed out an introduction briefed by Ros, and then we posted them off in batches when we passed a post office. Ros minded Barnaby while I played my part.

Often we were camped in beach-side caravan parks or camping grounds where Barnaby, who was a social little boy, would wander off and be invited into caravans by grandmothers missing their grandkids and plied with soft drinks and biscuits. We worried a bit at first about where he might be, but he always seemed to make his way back to our camp, so we became more relaxed about his absences, although sometimes we had to go looking for him.

These were very happy times. In mid-life it is sometimes difficult to find the time for this sort of travel, but as things turned out I was grateful for the bestial behaviour of the unspeakable Russell Warner at ABC Current Affairs Radio for giving us the opportunity to spend seven months exploring northern Australia. And when I did get back to Radio Drama & Features the following year, my ABC career was able to take a very different direction which also involved Ros, who eventually became my boss until she sacked me. But more of that later.

We continued to explore the east coast of Australia, taking every opportunity to leave the main highway to head to seaside national parks and other splendid locations. That was how we discovered Cape Hillsborough National Park to the east of Mackay in Northern Queensland, where we spent a week in our extended camping mode in our large marquee tent and while Ros searched for colourful characters to send off to the ABC in Sydney. Our camp site looked down over a tropical beach where kangaroos had taken to hopping along in the shallow water for reasons we never fathomed. Perhaps they just wanted to cool off, but it was a wondrous sight. One day, when Ros visited the bathroom and toilet complex Cape Hillsborough she heard a strange sound – an unknown man reciting poetry in the gents toilet.

This is how we met Percy Tresize, an engaging septuagenarian who used to ride his bicycle once a year down to Sydney (and back to Mackay) to perform in the Sydney Eisteddfod poetry performance section. It turned out Percy found the acoustics in the dunny perfect for rehearsing his repertoire. He was certainly a very fit old bloke. I recall Ros took a photo of him on the beach dressed as Old Father Time carrying a full-sized scythe.

Ros recorded him in action in the dunny (I guarded the door of the Gents to ensure Ros' privacy), as well as the details of his annual pilgrimage. Percy usually did well at the Eisteddfod and had a string of awards to prove it.

Our 'Farthest North' was Cooktown, which abounded with colourful characters who yielded a rich harvest for Ros' radio interview, before we returned to Cairns and headed south on the Kennedy Highway to join the Flinders Highway at Hughenden, and on to Broken Hill.

By this time we had been on the road for five of our seven months, and weather was starting to warm up towards the end of October. I decided that Mt Isa would probably be the last chance to edit Ros' tapes before heading for Darwin, and that was certainly the case. We booked into a caravan park in the Isa, and Ros put Barnaby into a day-care kindergarten to give me space to splice and edit the last of her interviews.

It was stinking hot, and I found great difficulty in getting the white sticky editing tape to adhere to the quarter-inch magnetic tape, not helped by my sweaty fingers. This was certainly going to be the last hurrah for sending Ros' magazine items to Sydney, but thankfully by them she had made us enough loot to finance the rest of the expedition.

When Ros went to pick up Barnaby at the end of the day, she found him gasping and dehydrated. There was water available from a bubbler which the other kids knew about, but he had never used one in his life and none of his carers at the kindergarten thought to show him how to work it! After all he was only two years old. Happily a few drinks of cold water did the trick in the late afternoon, but it could have led to quite serious dehydration.

We turned north for a brief period on the Barkly Highway out of Mt Isa which quickly swung to the west and Camooweal, the last town in Queensland, before crossing the border into The Northern Territory and reaching the aptly named Three Ways in the middle of nowhere really, but just north of Tennant Creek. There are three choices. Go back the way you came or head south to Alice Springs or north to Darwin. We chose to turn right aware that it was getting late in the year and the wet season was approaching. At least there was fuel available at Three Ways. We took a photo of Gertie and our modest trailer dwarfed by one of the enormous road trains with four linked trailers behind their prime movers that plied the Stuart Highway.

Pre rainy season clouds and steamy humidity greeted us as we approached Darwin in late November. We decided to camp at Curtin Springs which had two shallow freshwater reservoirs which could be used as swimming pools. We hoped to be able to cool off in them, but they were luke-warm and useless for lowering our body temperatures when we stood up to our necks in them, holding Barnaby with his head above water so he could still breathe. But it was hardly refreshing.

From time to time we would drive into the central city area of Darwin and find an airconditioned pub with where we could enjoy a beer and feel human again. The Darwin pubs were very good about tourists taking young kids into bars. Ros and I would make all kinds of plans of what we might do and where we might go, all of which collapsed into a sweaty heap as soon as we went back outside.

We only lasted a week, and decided to head south to Tasmania where we planned to join the Bowden family for Christmas on the East Coast near the town or Orford where my father John Bowden had built a vertical weather board weekender which looked straight out to sea over a dazzling white sandy beach towards the peaks of Maria Island - first named by the Dutch explorer Abel Tasman when he visited the south of Tasmania in 1642 naming it Van Diemens Land, and was the first explorer to confirm that Australia (then named New Holland) was an island continent.

My father had named the weekender *Askelon* after the town (spellings vary) on the shores of the Mediterranean in Palestine where he was posted during World War II. He described it as a wooden shack with million dollar views, and he was absolutely right. To get there meant a long drive right across the continent, and the Stuart Highway in those days was a goat track in comparison with today, and unsealed just south of Alice Springs until the South Australian border. The so-called highway had treacherous traps of red 'bulldust' which meant a slow and cautious approach. Of course the road trains caused them, and I had to keep a cautious eye on the rear vision mirror to make sure we pulled well off the road when a road train loomed up trailing a plume of red dust that could be seen 20 kilometres away.

Barnaby took all this in his stride, sitting between us in the front seat in his baby seat, and taking in the sights and experiences of outback travel, although in later life he gave us a hard time for travelling with him through all this exciting country when he was too young to remember anything about it!

The distance by road from Darwin to Melbourne (where we planned to catch the vehicular ferry the *Spirit of Tasmania* across Bass Strait to Devonport) is some 3,740 kilometres, which with some rest days along the way, was to take us three weeks. It was fortunate we left Darwin when we did, because some four weeks later, on Christmas Eve, Cyclone Tracy, literally blew the old Darwin away!

It seemed catastrophes were to dog us wherever we went in 1974 and early 1975, and fortunately we were safely at Spring Beach, at *Askelon*, just south of Orford, when on the evening of 5 January the bulk ore carrier *Lake Illawarra* crashed into some of the pylons of the Tasman Bridge -

collapsing a large section of the roadway, which connected the city of Hobart with the Eastern Shore of the Derwent River including the suburbs of Bellerive and Lindisfarne. It was an accident that never should have happened, but then again that is true of all accidents if they could have been foreseen I guess.

This one was bizarre and happened at 9.30 pm on a foggy night. The *Lake Illawarra* was carrying 10,000 tonnes of zinc ore concentrate to offload its cargo to the Risdon Zinc Works some three kilometres upstream from Hobart. The ship was off course when it approached the main central navigation span of the 45 metre high bridge, partly because of the strong tidal current, but also of the inattention of its captain Boleslaw Pele. Initially approaching the bridge at eight knots, Pele slowed the ship to a 'safe' speed. Although the *Lake Illawarra* was capable of passing through the bridge's central navigation span, the captain elected to pass through one of the narrower eastern spans.

Despite several changes of course, the ship proved unmanageable due to the strength of the current. In desperation the captain ordered full speed astern, at which point all control was lost. The out-of-control bulk carrier drifted towards the bridge, midway between the central navigation span and the eastern shore, crashing into three of the supporting pylons, bringing three unsupported bridge spans which crashed down into the river and on to the ship's deck which sank within minutes in 35 metres of water, trapping and drowning seven members of the crew.

Mercifully traffic on the bridge was light at that time of night, and no cars were actually on the section of roadway that collapsed. However all the lights on the bridge had failed at the time of the accident. Four cars drove over the edge into the gap, killing five occupants. Two drivers managed to stop their vehicles at the edge of the chasm, but not before their front wheels had actually dropped over the lip of the bridge deck. One of these cars contained Sylvia and Frank Manley.

Sylvia, in the front passenger seat, thought there had been an accident, and Frank who was driving, slowed down to 40 km/h. Sylvia was peering

Barnaby checking out his bedroom over the Kombi engine.

Gertie chose this spot right outside the Normanton Council Chambers in outback Queensland for her speedo to clock up 100,000 miles.

ahead trying to see what was happening. Then she said to Frank, 'The bridge is gone'!

Frank hit the brakes as Sylvia said, 'The white line has gone. Stop!' Frank hit the brakes, but said, 'I can't stop! I can't stop!' Their car hung precariously over the gap. Sylvia swung her door open and could see down to the water, so she swung herself towards the back seat of the car. 'There's a big automatic transmission pan under the car and that's what it balanced on.'

The other car also with its front wheels over the edge of the gap contained Murray Ling, his wife Helen and two of their children. Ling had a premonition that something was wrong and slowed down. He then noticed several cars ahead of him seemingly disappear as they drove over the edge. A following car, it's driver caught unawares by the unexpected stop, drove into the rear of Ling's car, pushing its front wheels over the breach. He eased his family out of the car, then stood horrified as two other cars ignored his attempts to wave them down as they raced past, one of which actually swerved around to avoid him and hurtled over the edge down into the River Derwent. The driver of a bus full of people did take notice of Ling's frantic signalling and swerved and skidded, slamming into the side railing of the bridge, so saving the lives of his passengers.

A total of 12 people died in the disaster. Seven crew of the MV *Lake Illawarra* and five motorists.

The bridge collapse had seriously disrupted the lives of Hobart's residents which had heavily relied upon it for most daily activities, including Hobart's two major hospitals. Some 30 per cent of Hobart's residents lived on the eastern shore and were only serviced by a few clinics. The next morning when 30,000 eastern shore residents set out for work they found that their former three-minute commute over the bridge had turned into a 90 minute drive up minor roads on the eastern shore to Bridgewater, the next available crossing of the Derwent, and down the western shore to the city. Ferry services had been organised and started by the next morning and continued until a temporary two-lane Bailey bridge two kilometres up the river was opened a year later and the Tasman Bridge was repaired and was back in service in three years in 1977.

. . . .

We had a painless trip back to Sydney from Hobart on a direct vehicular ferry service available in early 1975, but not for much longer, to resume real life. Me back at the ABC but now in the Department of Radio Drama & Features having rowed my refugee's boat across William St from Current Affairs Radio and its unspeakable supremo, Russell Warner to a more congenial atmosphere where I was able to explore making long-form radio documentaries and start what came to be known as the Social History Unit in which Ros played a pivotal part.

Ros and I had signed up, after Barnaby's adoption, to a second child which entailed a statutory two-year wait. But as if to give credence to Bob Dylan's great song, *The Times They are A' Changin'* were exceedingly apt where it came to adoption. The most significant was the introduction of the Supporting Mothers' Benefit by the Whitlam Labor Government in 1973.

The supporting mother's benefit legislation introduced in 1973 by the Whitlam government. It was a welfare payment given to mothers who didn't qualify for the existing widows pension. This was a turning point because it provided women with the means to choose to raise their children without a father figure. In the early 1970s, Australia's Female Liberation movement began to win sweeping advances for women's rights because of a range of policy reforms. One of these was the Supporting Mothers' Benefit which was awarded to never married mothers and other types of mothers who were not eligible for the Widow's Pension.

Before 1973, the process of getting a pension or any financial aid from the state was immensely complicated and impossible. The Widows Pension provided the largest amount of welfare and concessions, but it was only available to women who had been divorced, deserted or widowed. Unmarried women who were raising their children alone faced based difficult choices, often involving the traumatic relinquishment of the child for adoption or working long hours to support them. The introduction of the Supporting Mothers Benefit was a significant event in the Female

Liberation Movement because it provided women with further control over their bodies and their lives especially in relation to the children. This reduced the number of adoptions, social stigma towards single parents and helped abolish the legal concept of legitimacy. The supporting mother's benefit was introduced to reduce the number of adoptions.

In the western world, adoption was the solution to the growing problem of illegitimate children and single motherhood. In the late 1960s and early 1970s the amount of legal adoptions peaked. It was intensely traumatising. Birth mothers often experienced a high incidence of grief which often intensified over time. The lack of financial support played a role in helping convince women to relinquish their child. The success of adoption was built on the grim prophecies that depicted single women raising their children as being condemned to living in poverty and despair.

Unmarried mother's were not only economically deprived but we are also stigmatised by society at a time when the survival of single mothers and their children depended on their silence. Women who had children out of wedlock were perceived as stupid or selfish. In some cases unmarried mothers were kept in separate wards at hospitals in case they might upset married mothers awaiting the birth of their children.

The Whitlam Government's timely legislation did much to reduce the stigma on unwed mothers and enabled them to keep their children. So it was not surprising that the time previously calculated to allow us a second adoption had stretched.

There was also the added influence of what was known as Operation Babylift, the name given to the mass evacuation of children from South Vietnam to numerous countries across the world including Australia.

On 22 March 1975, the Saigon Post newspaper reported that the United States was beginning to airlift 10,000 refugees a day from the central Vietnam city of Da Nang. Australia also began airlifting orphans from April 1975.

Some saw Operation Babylift as a humanitarian act, while others were concerned about the future of these Asian children in Australia.

Tragically, the first plane bound for the United States crashed only twelve minutes after take-off. Some 143 babies and volunteers were killed, including two Australians from Adelaide, who had volunteered to help with the children. This tragedy, however, did not deter the operation from continuing. Some 3000 orphans were evacuated from Vietnam during April 1975.

Despite the Whitlam Government's timely pension for unmarried mothers, and indeed the sudden influx of Vietnamese orphans, some Australian-born children were still available for adoption. So it was that in July 1975 we had a phone call from Social Services saying that a baby boy was available, and that a social worker would call on us soon to assess our house, our progress with Barnaby, and interview us about our preparedness for the arrival of our second son. The understanding was that the social worker would not advise us of her visit ahead of time. This was three years on from Barnaby's arrival when he was all of nine days old!

When she did arrive to assess us the timing was, potentially, disastrous. The previous day I had offered a bevy of ABC colleagues one of whom had organised the delivery of two massive barrels of red wine, to use our Northbridge address as a bottling station. We had a raised car port which could be used to siphon the wine into bottles, and a merry day was had by all. Not all the wine made it into the bottles, and some were not in a fit state to drive home. It was decided we would move the cases of recently corked reds into our dining/living room to be collected the next day or so.

Ros also chose the next day to ask some women friends to lunch on our deck, adjacent to the temporary vino storage. The whole house reeked of booze from the wall to wall cases of bottled vino, and it has to be said that Ros and her friends were also in a fairly merry state as they were enjoying their lunch.

Of course the social worker chose that moment to arrive to interview us about our impending adoption!

I explained the situation as best I could, and the social worker seemed amiable enough despite having arrived in the den of what could be construed as Alcoholics Synonymous. But it was a great relief when the phone rang again a week later and a date was fixed for us to collect Guy Philip Bowden from the Crown Street Womens' Hospital in Redfern and a little brother for Barnaby John Bowden.

Although we collected Barnaby from Crown Street Hospital nine days after he was born, Guy was three weeks old when we brought him to 11 Marana Rd. Northbridge.

We were very lucky to get him. His birth mother was from a Catholic family, and I seem to recall that in the information Social Services allowed us to see, she had asked that her unborn son should go to a Catholic family. The social worker dealing with her case said they had found a couple they thought ideal for her baby, but they were not Catholic. Happily the birth mother said, 'Oh well then if you think they are the best choice for my son never mind about Catholicism'. Or words to that effect.

Ros had been scheduled to present and narrate her first edition of the pioneering feminist program *The Coming Out Show* on ABC Radio 2 (as it was then known – later Radio National) that afternoon. I said she should go ahead and do it, as I was perfectly capable of looking after our second son on his first day in his new home.

It has to be said I was a bit out of practise and should have doubled folded his nappy – this was before throw-away paper ones – and about 4 pm that afternoon when a neighbour kindly called to see how I was getting on, her arrival was timely. I had been trying to heat Guy's feeding bottle on the stove, just as Guy shat through his loose nappy all down the front of my shirt and corduroy trousers, just as the hot water began to boil over on the stove, overheating Guy's milk bottle. Norma came quickly to the rescue, and things were back on track when Ros arrived back home from the ABC.

. . . .

A year later, with Barnaby at pre-school and Guy able to be minded for a modest fee by an obliging neighbour, Ros was able to do some part-time work. A friend we knew in the Department of Immigration alerted us to new source of income for Ros. In the late 1970s, this organisation had begun a scheme to attract more migrants to the Land of Oz by having freelance journalists interview former migrants who had made good Down Under and were prepared to say so. These stories (with a photo) were only 500 words or so but were then translated into the language of the subject's homeland and published in local newspapers overseas.

Now Ros had trained as a nurse, but was certainly versatile. She went out and recorded interviews with the happy migrants and took the obligatory photographs. I helped her in the early stages with shaping the stories, but she soon picked up the basics and learned to use a typewriter to transcribe the audio interviews and indeed write her own stories. The Immigration Department paid quite generously for these contributions which was a great help to our family finances.

In the meantime Ros honed her burgeoning radio skills by volunteering to join Radio 2SER, a community radio station in Sydney which began broadcasting in October 1979 with studios operating in Ultimo, and on the campus of Macquarie University.

In the meantime, having rowed my refugee's boat across William Street away from the bestial ministrations of my bete noir the unlovely Russell Warner at Radio Current Affairs. I was welcomed into the fold of the Radio Drama & Features Department, which apart from commissioning writers who wrote radio plays, and then hiring actors to read the scripted dialogue, there was also a features branch which had as its showcase a Sunday night program titled *Sunday Night Radio 2* (which would later morph into *Radio National.* It ran from 7.15 in the evening to 10 pm. RD & F's Director, Richard (Dick) Connolly, was a classical scholar and later changed the name of the eclectic Sunday night offerings to *Radio Helicon.* Apparently Helicon in Greek mythology was a mountain where the muses gathered…

Ros and I combined to record and broadcast interviews with five contrasting Australians who had lived exciting and contrasting lives with the overall title of *On Their Own Terms.* Ros' first interview was with Mary Edgeworth David, who was born in 1888 and was the youngest daughter of Sir William Edgeworth David the eminent geologist and Antarctic explorer, and as Ros would find out, a strong single woman in an era when daughters were supposed to marry and have children.

Mary Edgeworth-David in her nineties when interviewed by Ros Bowden.

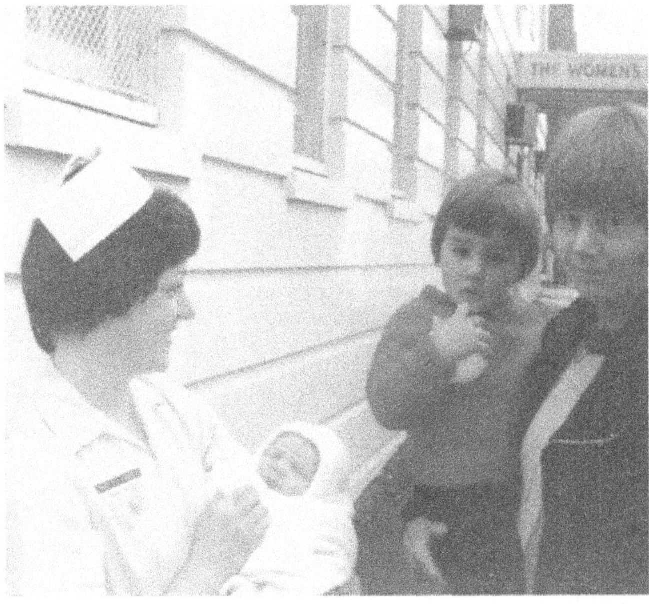

Three years after Barnaby was handed over outside the Crown Street Hospital to his new family it was Guy's turn. Barnaby seems a bit pensive.

But that was not on Mary Edgworth David's agenda. Here is part of a transcript of Ros' interview with her in 1975. She died in 1987 one year short of her 100th birthday.

. . . .

Ros: I remember Mary Edgeworth David when I was a child. When what we recall now as the alternative lifestyle was even thought about. Mary Edgeworth David was working to make herself self-sufficient. For example she installed the first solar hot water system that I had ever seen. And she even made her own self-knitted jumpers spun from the wool of her own sheep. And all this in suburban Sydney. It should be said that she began life under privileged circumstances. Her father was Sir Edgeworth David the scientist and Antarctic explorer, and her mother was the Chief Girl Guide of New South Wales. Her first book was a biography of her father and she recently completed her autobiography, *Passage of Time* at the age of 84. She was brought up in times when a girl's behaviour was rigidly defined – restrictions, which the young Mary refused to acknowledge. The maxim that ruled the young girl's life was that it would be considered unladylike.

MED: As a matter of fact we never thought of women's rights in my young days, we considered ourselves the equal of our men friends and nobody ever questioned it.

Ros: Do you remember the Suffragette Movement and the early feminist activism?

MED: Yes I do, I remember the whole family was quite worried about it. I don't know whether we altogether approved of them.

Ros: What about you yourself? Did you feel any sympathy with them?

MED: Yes I certainly did. But it seemed to me that the chaining themselves to railings and so on weren't going to do much good. I couldn't see the point of that.

Ros: Did your own career suffer because of the restrictions placed on women?

MED: I didn't have a career, so how could it? It never occurred to me that I would be anything but sort of part of my parents' home really. In those days an unmarried daughter just stayed at home and did housework. I drove the car and that was an interest in my life because I also looked after it. Cleaning the cylinder heads and grinding valves and things by myself. It wasn't until I had my own home and started doing things on my own here like mixing cement and getting a big tank and a nice base with blocks of sandstone for the tank to stand on that I used to feel slightly sheepish, I think, about mixing cement and doing men's work. And I always had a slightly guilty feeling that I shouldn't be doing men's work. Because I knew that men would think that I was silly and was probably doing it badly. There was that feeling that because you were a woman, anything you did in the men's line, would be silly and inadequate.

ROS: In your own family surroundings and amongst your own friends, were you ever stopped doing something because it was man's work and in men's interests.?

MED: Certainly not by my family. When we were fairly small we used to go up to Woodford for holidays and we lived in the bush there. We ran around with bare feet and my mother dressed my sister and me in trousers and blouses. Small boys sort of outfits. (Laughs.) Which rather shocked the people at the local boarding house. When we were in our teens my sister and I used to shock our girlfriends because our mothers would not let us wear corsets, bone corsets. She said they were unhealthy and women had been known to have their livers cut into by them. (Laughs.) Which was rather an exaggeration I think, but anyway we were not allowed to. Some people thought it was shocking that you could dance with a man and he could feel your back instead of the stays with his hand. (Laughs.)

Ros: You were lucky enough not to wear the clothes that other girls did at that time but what did you wear?

MED: Oh girls wore long skirts down to their ankles with voluminous petticoats. That meant quite a lot of washing and ironing because the petticoats were frilly with lots of tucks in them with the skirt on top and then they would have a belt and a blouse tucked in at the waist with 'leg-of-mutton' sleeves and hard straw hats pinned to their hair with long hairpins. Hairpins did come in handy for one niece of mine because she found that reading in bed at night in the winter time in Tasmania was very cold and the hairpin came in very handy for turning the pages of the book she was reading and wouldn't have to put her hand out from under the bed clothes. (Laughs.) So they had their uses.

Ros: Did they do the gardening with the long skirts on?

MED: When we grew up do you mean? No, we used to run through the bush with shirts and shorts. But when you reached the age of long skirts you were more sedate in your habits. You wouldn't do that because it would be considered unladylike.

Ros: Did that being lady like or unladylike worry you much?

MED: No, it didn't worry us at all really, but other people used to make catty remarks about us sometimes. I remember stepping over some ropes, or something, in a ferry boat when we were watching a college boat race and my mother was spoken to about my awful unlady-like behaviour because I had stepped over some ropes in order to get a better view. That was the sort of thing that happened to us kids. When I was quite a small girl about twelve I was shouted at by a navvy who was working on a railway line up at Woodford, Saying why didn't I ride side-saddle 'like a decent girl' instead of straddling my legs on each side. This upset me very much, so I got out my mother's old side-saddle which was much too big for the pony, and put it on, and I went down to the village and a horse and cart was coming along behind me as I stopped at the village store. When I got off, the side-saddle which was very loose slipped off with me and I was just about to tighten it when the pony shot out its hind leg and kicked me in the chest, and I fell to the ground unconscious, so that was one effect my unladylike behaviour head had on me.

Ros: What about going to school?

MED: Well I went to school in Burwood which was close to Ashfield. We only went there for one year and I didn't like it at all. So after that my sister and I had a governess. My brother, of course, had to go to a boys school.

Ros: I guess you didn't see your father as much as your mother because your father was living in the city during the week, and only came home at weekends. But what sort of influences did he have on you?

MED: Well he had a great influence on our literary tastes, because he always read aloud to us in the evenings, and it was always good stuff. Sir Walter Scott and all those historical novels and he was also very keen on poetry and we used to love the evenings when he read. I always remember one occasion – my mother was not at all politically minded – she was very practical, and I remember one evening when father was reading Lord Alfred Tennyson's *Crossing the Bar*, and he was very moved by the poem and so were we children. We were hanging on his words and at the end there was a pause, and we were all sort of recovering from this moving experience, and my mother's voice piped up and said: 'I think we will have that cold lamb made into an Irish stew for dinner tonight'. And he was not at all impressed by that.

Ros: What other influences did he have on you? Did he enjoy the outdoor life with you?

MED: Yes he did, he was a very good out-of-doors person. But I felt he never really chopped wood, as a man who had been brought up to it. He would chop it, but he complained that it jarred his arms. Well a really experienced woodcutter doesn't actually grasp the axe firmly when it hits the wood. And we became expert in that at a very early age. (Laughs.)

Ros: Were motorcars very evident at that time in Sydney?

MED: No, there weren't any, not up in the mountains when we were children. But I do remember my first ride in one, It was when I was about 16 and I was sent to boarding school at that time to be disciplined. Some elderly friends called one afternoon to see me and got permission to take me for a ride in their motorcar. It was a thrilling experience although a little frightening, and we sat in the body of the car whilst they sat on a seat that was pulled up at the back so you were looking at one another across the interior instead of facing the engine.

Ros: When you were a girl and perhaps some years after that 'Coming Out' was very important for a young woman. Do you remember that custom?

MED! Oh yes, we all had to come out at Government House dances that was the thing to do. I remember that a niece of my neighbour protested she didn't want to come out at Government House, because she didn't want to dance with men aged thirty! And she wasn't far wrong because there weren't very many young men invited to those dances.

Ros: Did you yourself come out and do you remember it?

MED: Yes I do. And I remember one of the matrons at Government House asking me at one time did I have plenty of dance of partners? And being very truthful, and not at all tactful, said, 'No not very many'. (Laughs.) And she looked displeased and turned to the Aide next to her, and said, 'Please see that Miss David has plenty of partners to dance with'.

Ros: What was the city of Sydney like early in the century?

MED: Well it was a very nice, small, friendly place and on Saturday mornings practically everyone from the surrounding suburbs would stroll around in the city and do a little shopping and always have either coffee and cakes at the Civil Service refreshment room in Market Street. And practically next door to the Civil Service store in Market Street was Washingtons the chemist with a wonderful soda fountain where young people to used to meet and enjoy Ice-cream Sodas which were just coming in at that time. Delicious things.

Ros: What about the cultural life of the city, where there are many art galleries and theatres?

MED: There were always theatres of course, two or three, which used to put on reasonably good comedies and so on, and there was one art gallery because I don't think there was the same interest in art in those days that there is now. Now there is more business interest, as people buy up expensive pictures as an asset for when times were going to be hard.

Ros: What about visiting artists from overseas?

Yes, we used to have people like Madame Pavlova, then in the twilight of her career, and we used to occasionally had male actors but not very often.

Ros: They must have come to Australia in a long trip by boat.

MED: Yes they did, but they enjoyed it I think because actors and actresses always went First Class. I remember that because the children always went Second Class on the boats. And we were sometimes taken to a fancy-dress ball in the Second Class and the celebrity actresses from First Class would do the judging of the costumes.

Ros: I guess there was a lot of class consciousness then was there not?

MED: I don't know – our family never suffered from it! (Laughs.)

Ros: Did you look on it as a disease?

MED: No, we thought it was something that belonged to the lower orders who were snobbish and snobbishness was something that the best people didn't go in for.

. . . .

Ros' interview with the formidable Aboriginal social worker Shirley Smith, always known as 'Mum Shirl' was in stark contrast to the aristocratic Mary Edgeworth David.

Ros: Very few people live more *On Their Own Terms* than Mrs Shirley Smith better known as Mum Shirl. She is epileptic, illiterate and black and she functions most efficiently as a one-woman welfare agency and counselling service in the inner suburbs of Sydney. From her base with the priests and nuns at the Convent of Mercy in Redfern she involves herself with poor blacks, visiting jails or representing them in court. She constantly helps unmarried mothers which is one of the main purposes behind the Aboriginal Legal and Medical Services. Her method of operating is highly individualistic to say the least. People call into the Convent to get her personal help and advice and she is just as likely to offer them her bed for the night if they don't have a place to sleep. Mum Shirl's working hours often go around the clock and she is so constantly on the move it was something of an achievement to pin her down long enough to record this interview at the Convent in Redfern.

The redoubtable Shirley Smith, 'Mum Shirl', interviewed by Ros for the ABC radio documentary *On Their Own Terms*.

MS: I was born an epileptic and I'm a controlled one now. The Mission I was born on was in Cowra. Most the Aboriginal men from the Cowra Mission worked at a place called Wyangala Dam and used to go there every day. And if the men wasn't working they used to go and keep the Mission streets clean and do odd jobs around the Managers house – keeping his garden nice, pruning his citrus trees and mowing his lawns and jobs like that. Aboriginal people never got the same treatment for the same wages as white people for what they did. We got rations twice a week, tea, sugar, onions and potatoes, flour, rolled oats and Cocky's Joy which was golden syrup. We sometimes got some plum jam. We were some of the most deprived people in the world. Because our parents, our mother wasn't paid child endowment, she was given a pink form to go to the store to buy food and she was given a Child Endowment Order, from the Aboriginal Protection Board.

Ros: Shirley Smith didn't have much idea what she wanted to do in life when she moved to with her parents to Sydney, aged 16. That was in 1937 and jobs were scarce enough for qualified whites. But for an illiterate, black, epileptic, woman paid employment was out of the question. Her elder brother whom she loved and admired was sent to gaol for a crime. And while he was there, she visited him and came in contact with other prisoners as well. First, she was just a sympathetic person to talk to, and someone who occasionally took in chocolates or cigarettes. Later she began carrying messages to prisoners' relatives. Being illiterate, she could not write these messages down but relied on her phenomenal memory. Once an educated German boy asked her to write a letter on his behalf, because he didn't trust the prison authorities.

MS: So he spoke the letter to me, 'Dear mum and dad, I'm in the jail somewhere in Australia', and he went on and said he was nicknamed 'Cat' and had a pet goat and gave details of his life at home – and I memorised every word. And then I got somebody to write that down. And he got an answer back because I asked his mother to write back to the prison. And when he got the letter, he waited for me to read the letter. Then I had a terrible bad time. Because I couldn't read – I couldn't read the letter. And

I said to the boy wouldn't it be nice if you got one of the prison officers here, and I called the officer by name and asked him because that old gentleman knew that I could not read and write. And he read the letter out to the boy who said to me 'Is that right what he is saying', and I said, 'Well would you like me to read it'. Because while the prison officer was reading that letter I listened very carefully and when I repeated it to the German boy there was not a thing I left out. Because at that time I had a terrible fear that I had let that boy down. It wasn't until six years later when he was extradited back to Germany to do his life sentence and I said, 'I have to tell you something'. And he said, 'What is it'? I said, 'The day you asked me to write a letter for you, I wished I could've been anywhere but with you'. He said, 'Why'? I said, 'Because I couldn't read and write'. And he said, 'But that is not true. I know you wrote my letters'. I said, If I had told you I couldn't read and write and had to memorise what you said for someone else to write down would you have believed me'? And he started laughing. He said, 'I suppose I wouldn't have'.

Ros: Have you learned to read and write yourself since then?

MS: Yes, I can read some words and if I don't know what a word is and I'm with a person I can trust I spell it out and the person will tell me what it is. And then I put it in my mind, and if I see the word again, I can read that word and remember it.

Ros: What sort of things did you do for the prisoners when you were going around the gaols?

MS: As I said, I could not read and write, but they would tell me about their mothers and fathers and girlfriends, brothers and sisters, and where he last knew where they lived, and I would memorise it. From the time I walked out of the prison and repeat it over and over in my mind what was said, what number in the street and where the house was.

Ros: What sort of crimes were these people in prison for?

MS: Well, loitering, vagrancy, and no fixed place of an abode notifications. And of course a lot was for assault and robbery, breaking and entering, illegal use, and a lot of young boys was picked up for they called it the milk run – people left out money for the milkman – so they would take the money and when they were in court they were charged with that. On the milk run, they would get three months, or if it was six months they would do four and a half. It all depended on whether they had a juvenile delinquent record.

Ros: And how much would they have to pinch to get a four-and-a-half months sentence?

MS: Three bottles of milk in 1942 or 1944, will when milk was only sixpence a bottle. Young Christine was only fourteen-and-a-half when she stole three bottles of milk and she got sentenced and sent to Parramatta Girls Industrial home and she was sent there until the superintendent gave her a recommendation or a report that she could come out. But that young girl done six-and-a-half months for three bottles of milk. I remember one case of a young boy who got three months for vagrancy. He went to Long Bay Gaol and he was sexually assaulted. And he was only a young boy, not quite 19. That young man is doing life today because he killed the man who sexually assaulted him.

Ros: Lack of communication with the outside world was one of the things that confirmed Mum Shirl's prison visits. She would deliver messages to anyone. Most of their own people were illiterate and must have suffered from not being able to contact their relatives. Prisoners who were white fellas also had a problem. The shame felt by their relatives because they were in gaol, and Mum Shirl took messages to them from their families too.

MS: If Mr and Mrs Jones lived in a smart Street in uptown Glebe or Balmain or Vaucluse and a letter comes to your place delivered by the postman, and it's got on it At Her Majestys Service, the envelopes were very thin and you could see the written word inside it, so the neighbours would know that they had a letter from the gaol. You see people who had a position in the community were churchgoers, they didn't want their relatives to write home from gaol. So there was no communication. Young kids in prison, had nothing to do, no one to write to or talk to. no one to see at visiting times and if they did have a visitor the parents used to say to the young prisoner, 'For God's sake don't write no more letters. It was a real embarrassment. I walked down the street and everybody was watching me. I told the neighbours that you've gone into the country for a holiday'. So in prison these boys just stick together and play cards talk, have conversations, and that is the only sort of contact they had and do you wonder why the kids come out of the gaol brainwashed.

Ros: Mum Shirl's prison work went beyond just visiting. In the end she was given authority with a special badge from the Department of Correctional Services to represent people in court. Of course she had no legal training but she had always been an astute observer. And once again, her memory was a great asset, because her reading and writing was still minimal. She began by helping prisoners like her brother, but she also developed an interest in all people who were in trouble. The old, the sick, unmarried mothers, the poor and the hungry. The aim was to use the system to help the under-privileged and the uneducated to get the help they were entitled to. I have listened to her talking on the telephone, and on the courtroom steps and her methods are all unorthodox but she obviously has the respect and affection of officials as well as the people she defends.

MS: On 16 March this year I've been doing this sort of work for 30 years and between those times I've been involved with unmarried mothers and alcoholics – my biggest problem I suppose was I was involved with a lot of people that I shouldn't have been. First of all, old people who didn't have enough food to eat, and often I could tell them how to work the system to get some. I used to go into the park and talk to them. Some of those people don't talk to dark people.

Ros: When you defended these people in court, how did you learn to stand up to smart lawyers?

MS: Well I went to a lawyer once, he was very young, but a very brilliant barrister, at the time, and I always call him, one of my greatest gifts, My privilege was to meet him in court and listen to how he worked and just for curiosity's sake I would sit up at the back in the gallery and look down, and think, 'My god, how could he defend a case as bad as this'? I'd see him writing on a piece of or blotter, and he would do tracks like he was doing crosswords. I didn't understand at that time until about after about six years after that that man had used these symbols as part and parcel of his defence of the person in court. And how he would tackle it using his symbols as memory joggers. And every time I knew that he was in Darlinghurst are used to sit there and listen to him conduct his court cases.

Ros: So you learned methods of defence and strategy in court from the experts?

MS: I think he was one of the greatest. And of course listening to judges, and then I came into my own I suppose. I had been a prison visitor and I worked very hard with that badge I now carry.

Ros: Can you tell me about the badge?

MS: It was like opening a book, and gave me the right to enter institutions including gaols and talk to prisoners not through their bars, but in their cells under the supervision of a warder.

Ros: So the pass gave you access into gaols, but what other powers did it have?

MS: Well if a young person goes to gaol I can go to court in spite of the Child Welfare Act which says there's nobody outside a mother and father or a grandparent and go to court for a child if they are under 18. But that badge gave me the power to stand up there and say, 'I'm Shirley Smith from the Department of Corrective Services and I'm talking here for so and so. And then I would sit down. A lot of police officers used to say to me, how come a black person, an Abo, got a pass from the department? And I said I worked stuffing hard for it.

Ros: In the early 1970s Mum Shirl became involved in what was known as the Breakfast Program. To make sure that underprivileged kids at least got to school with a full belly. The program has been absorbed into other schemes now but it's typical how Mum Shirl react positively to community problems.

MS: A girl of 13 years-of-age came to me one day and she said, 'I'm not going back to school no more'. And I thought that's a funny thing for a little girl so small to say. And I said, if you don't want to go back to school I want to know all about it. She said, 'My mother lives in Chippendale and she gets a pension which is not enough so she goes and does a couple of hours extra work sometimes when she can – like cleaning up an office. And she said, "Sometimes I don't have the money to go to Chippendale or King Street in Newtown or down to the junior school in Marrickville".' And I said, 'Will you tell me why you don't want to go to school'? 'No I don't want to go to school,' She said, 'When I do go to school the teacher tells me to wear a white blouse and to wear black shoes and stockings and I told her that my mother could not afford it. I didn't mind them laughing about me or talking about me at school. One of our lady school teacher said to me one day, "You're just a lazy brat. And all the money people are spending on you".' The little girl told me she couldn't understand that because no one was spending money on her, she said, 'Because my mother couldn't afford it'. So I said well we'd better go and see the school teacher. She said, 'I'm not going to school'. I said, 'Look my girl, we'll have to do it my way'. She said, 'But how can I concentrate on the blackboard and what the school teacher is talking about when I never had breakfast and I walked from Chippendale to Marrickville, and I'm just waiting for the bell to ring so I can go and pick up my food at the tuckshop which gets paid out of our endowment every month. I come home that hungry I have to pinch my belly so I don't sing out in school'. So I said, 'I'd like to talk to the school teacher'. Then I bought her a pair of shoes and socks and we went to the school teacher. And I said to her, 'Have you never wondered in your mind why Annette wasn't listening to you at school'? And she said no. No never. I said to Annette, 'Would you like to tell the lady now'? And she said, 'Why should I'? And I said, 'I want you to tell her'.

'Look miss, she said to the teacher, I didn't listen to you because I was so hungry from walking all the way from my place to here. And straightaway I saw a change come over that young schoolteacher's face – of disbelief. I said, 'Don't you believe the young girl'? She said, 'Well, it's a little bit far-fetched the things she said'. And I said, 'I don't think so'. I said, 'If you've been in the business I've been in for so long you can almost read people's faces'. I could see that she was telling me that she was treating

Annette on the same level as every European child or white person in that school. She didn't ring true to me.

Ros: So did the Breakfast Program follow on from that?

MS: The Breakfast Program was the greatest thing that the young black militants ever put up. The Reverend Ted Noffs came and spoke to me and I said, 'I'm flat to the boards with gaols and institutions, but how can I help'? So we involved the alcoholics, people who were addicted to drugs, helping them with a Breakfast Program in Holland Park, Newtown. A big new trailer used to go up there every morning with morning cereals and baked beans on toast, poached eggs, and if it was a bit cold we went to the Methodist Church in Newtown and from there, with the young girl by his side, the Rev Noffs talked about the underprivileged children in the suburbs of Sydney who couldn't afford to have breakfast. They were going to school and couldn't concentrate all the lessons because they was hungry. Well the clergyman at the Methodist Church gave us a property and renovated it, had it painted and bought a lovely new electric stove, sinks and toilets for the hungry kids. There were people there who would give them breakfast and then put them in cars and take them back to their schools.

Ros: I suppose one of the most remarkable things about Mum Shirl is her extraordinary capacity for work. She must be well into her 50s and despite her considerable bulk she never seems to stop. For example I talked to her at 8:30 pm one Wednesday night and ask her to tell me what she had been doing for the past 48 hours.

MS: I got up early and talked to white people, one was from Child Welfare, one was from the ABC and one was from Radio 2SM. Then I went to court for a person who was there for breaking entering and stealing, and I was able to get him on remand. I then talked to his parents, and where he used to work, or friends or anyone who could tell me something about his background and his life before I would become involved with him. This young boy wasn't an aboriginal, he was white and he just asked me if I would go to court for him, because he never had no money to pay a lawyer and he couldn't come under the Aboriginal Legal Service. So I went and talked on behalf of him. Then I went and done my ordinary work around the town in the suburbs near Redfern. I got a young priest to drive me to Erskineville, Marrickville and to Dulwich Hill, Lewisham, Stanmore then back to Newtown and back to Erskineville. By that time I was ready to get in the car with two seminarians to see a young boy who is going to court back in my own home town of Cowra, so we left Sydney I suppose about 8:30 am and got to Cowra a little after 2 am Tuesday morning and talked to my sister who was on the Mission they were born and bred on, and then I went to court. I was in town until 4.20 pm and in the evening I had something to eat and then we come back to Sydney about 12.45 in the morning. Then this morning I thought I was going to sleep in but somebody told me that I had messages in the book – which is a 24 hour service – and learned that I had to go to court at Redfern this morning for a young man who had assaulted his wife, and went to Redfern court and acted for him because he did not have a lawyer, and I had to leave the young man with the police officers because I had to go to the children's court in Albion Street. I thought I was going to court for one person, but it turned out to be three. I got out about 4 pm and I had had no lunch or breakfast. Two were charged up for illegal use of a motor vehicle, breaking and enter, young girl had a absconded from home, and placed herself in moral danger, I think overall between the time I got up Monday morning and the time I landed back at the Convent on Tuesday evening were the two busiest days in my life for the last seven years – because I had to go to two courts under two different judges and walked out with four people with their freedom.

4

Ros the Life Saver

Before Ros and I were blessed with our two adopted boys we always spend our Christmas holidays in Tasmania at my parents' beach cottage near Orford on the East Coast, with had a fantastic view out to sea with the peaks of Maria Island in the foreground. (After our boys were old enough to travel with us we still went to Tasmania for Christmas but our activities were not as robust before they arrived in 1972 and 1975).

Ros was not that keen on bushwalking, but did not mind day walks. And so it was that we drove our Kombi up into the highlands on a Hydro Electric Commission road built to give access to the dam that would eventually drown Lake Pedder, a jewel in the crown of Tasmanian high country that would soon disappear.

Now as a bush walker of some experience in Tasmania (my parents had bravely included me on the overland track from Lake St Clair to Cradle Mountain a walk of some 100 kilometres when I was ten years old) I knew that it was essential not to walk in shorts mainly because gaiters and long trousers were a defence against Tasmania's native Tiger snakes which were deadly if they bit you on unprotected flesh, as they had unusual fangs, which did not inject their poison through the fangs, but the venom ran down a groove on the upper part of the fangs, and there was a good chance the venom would be wasted on the fabric of the gaiters and long trousers.

As a matter of fact the deadly effectiveness of the Tiger snake had impressed itself into my 10-year-old brain during our 1948 bush walk when there had been a young woman bitten under bizarre circumstances which is a story worth telling and a lead in to how Ros undoubtedly saved my life near Lake Pedder in 1971.

In the summer of 1948 we had to carry everything with us on our backs of course – tents, food and cooking gear. Not water, because there was always plenty of that in the Tasmanian wilderness. It seems hard to comprehend these days, plastic containers yet to be invented. We had cylindrical aluminium containers with screw lids scammed from chemist shops – they were ideal for food storage, and waterproof. We carried rice, rolled oats, dried food and even tea in cloth bags. Rucksacks were very primitive, suspended on a metal a shaped frame and leather strap the load stayed back making the damned things twice as heavy as they should be. In those days only a handful of eccentric's went to bushwalking. You certainly didn't expect to meet anyone else on the track, in normal circumstances you would reasonably expect to have the wilderness on your own.

I dictated an account of our trip because my Aunt Nora Bowden, was a shorthand typist and transcribed it and typed it out later. It was my first attempt at oral history, I suppose, with myself as the narrator and references to 'the womenfolk' doing this and that and rather formal police-style talk. We often 'proceeded' along the track rather than walked. Most hikers these days begin from Cradle Mountain in the north and walk south to Lake St Clair, but we did it from the south. We started on New Year's Day, getting a lift to Derwent Bridge on the service car – a large sedan or small bus which did the milk run Queenstown on the West Coast, carrying papers, mail, general cargo and some passengers, stopping at Derwent Bridge near Lake St Clair on the way

'We got into the service car and we heard that the driver had been drinking beer and sherry until 4 o'clock that morning morning. We felt very encouraged as you may imagine. The driver drove very fast and it was very dangerous'.

The main road to the West Coast was an unsealed, potholed corrugated goat track, but one bonus of starting from Lake St Clair end was that you could organise a boat to save you the first day's walk to the head of the lake walk. Our 10 day trip was not without incident. We got lost trying to find an allegedly idyllic high mountain plateau called The Labyrinth and had to scrub bash down into a valley to spend an unscheduled night. (I did eventually get to the Labyrinth a decade later and it was truly magnificent, little lakes and wind-sculptured King Billy Pines surrounded by mountain peaks with classical names like The Acropolis and Mount Eros).

We were only a day away from Cradle Mountain, our journeys end, and we were resting beside the track enjoying a restorative ration of chocolate looking up to a great sweep of country towards a mountain called Barn Bluff, we heard the unmistakable sound of someone running. A young man without a haversack, was thundering along the and ran up to us with the terrible news that a young woman had been bitten by a snake near Pelion Hut, a days walk back, and he was on his way to raise the alarm and get a doctor from Sheffield, the nearest major town.

The circumstances of the accident were bizarre. A young woman was walking with a small group of male mainland university students. She dropped behind her group to have a piddle. Unfortunately, a Tiger snake was on the other side of the log she chose for her buttocks support, and it reared up and bit her twice on her nether regions. The Tasmanian Tiger snake is listed as one of the most poisonous snakes in the world.

But it does not inject its venom into its prey, and its poison runs down a groove in its fangs. The young woman made light of the incident, believ-ing that the snake was unlikely to be poisonous. But all Tasmanian snakes are venomous and that is why bushwalkers always wear long trousers and gaiters. Should a snake strike, there was a good chance most of the venom would be soaked up in the material and not be fatal. But it was only when she collapsed that the true state of affairs was known. Of course due to the intimate area of the snake bite, a tourniquet was not possible. The young men carried her to the Pelion Hut and one of their party began running 20 kilometres along the track to try and get help. He met Graham Mar-shall, another climber who had just climbed Cradle Mountain that day but who agreed to run on towards the settlement at Cradle Mountain where there was a telephone. Marshall had run another eight kilometres when he caught up with us.

The first aide treatment in those days was to put on the tourniquet (if possible). cut the wound with a little scalpel, suck out the poison (difficult under the circumstances) and pour purple coloured Condys Crystals over the affected area. We carried the same kits housed in little wooden cylinders. Later results proved these snake-bite kits were totally useless. The only hope for snake bite-victims – other than to survive through good luck – was to be injected with an anti-venene, which was not an option. By the time we reached *Waldheim* the lodge at the entrance to the park, we met the doctor and the police party on their way in from the town of Sheffield. The doctor told us that the young woman would either be alive or dead. Sadly, she had died during the night in the Pelion Hut.

I put in the diary I dictated to Aunt Nora that the police had come out to arrest the snake.

Back to 1971, and because Ros and I were walking in high mountain country with low scrubby shrubs and unusually hot dry weather, we were both wearing shorts – despite the precautions we should have been taking. I was telling Ros a fantastic anecdote about something-or-other and had just reached the punch-line, when Ros suddenly and unexpectedly pushed me sideways just as I was stepping over a log, and I realised that I had come within a millisecond of stepping on a large Tiger snake sunning itself on the ground on the other side of the fallen branch I was about to straddle. A re-run of the fate of that poor young woman in 1948 might well have repeated itself for me if the observant Ros had not taken the instant aggressive action she had!

I never wore shorts again when bushwalking in Tasmania.

. . . .

It's a sign of an octogenarian failing memory I suppose, that I can't recall exactly how the concept of forming the Social History Unit (SHU) under the auspices of my new association with the Department of Radio Drama & Features came about in 1975. I do remember that a producer Daniel Connell (who had been seconded to the National Papua New Guinea Broadcasting Corporation from the ABC's Radio Education Department for several years and had recently returned to Sydney) had recorded some seminal interviews on his own volition with leading Papua New Guinean figures including the Governor Sir John Guise, the long-serving Prime Minister Michael Somare, Sir Maori Kiki, Dame Rachel Cleland the wife of an early Assistant Administrator in 1915, Sir Donald Cleland, Bernard

Ros at the Walls of Jerusalem shortly before saving my life by pushing me sideways as I was about to step on a tiger snake with bare legs.

Marius Webb, one of the founders of the ABC's ground-breaking rock music radio stations in 2013. Later he became the ABC's Head of Personnel (which he referred to as The Controller of Human Happiness).

Narakobi, veteran politician and jurist, and more – comprising some 30 hours of audio.

Ros Bowden came on board as a freelance and immediately started to do some remarkable work. Her six-part series titled *Being Aboriginal* won her the first Human Rights Award ever presented for radio in 1978.

(I never won a prize for any of my radio documentaries recorded over many years!)

Stephen Rapley was seconded from the Talks Department, and Bill Bunbury contributed enthusiastically from Perth in Western Australia although technically still working for the about to-be dismantled Radio Education Department. I was designated as the Executive Producer of SHU, and we were given two weekly slots to fill on Radio 2. *Talking History* (immediately nicknamed *Squawking Mystery* by Bill Bunbury) was a half hour magazine program showcasing oral history interviews and associated issues and we also began a weekly 15-minute interview program *Word of Mouth* which could be a one-off interview, or episodic.

Enter Marius Webb who had been one of the two co-ordinators of the ground-breaking new youth radio outlet from the ABC, Double Jay, in the dying days of the Whitlam Labor Government in 1975. One of Double Jay's two co-ordinators the youthful Marius cut a dashing figure topped by a luxuriant explosion of frizzy hair as he and his co-ordinator Ron Moss began to shake up the youth oriented music industry. Announcer Chris Winter explained at the time, that there was an enormous breadth of music around at the time 'that was not played on radio, but could be heard in private gatherings or bought from specialist stores'. The original aim of Double J was to highlight 'our own culture' and the staff were expected to 'provide an alternative to the mainstream, with a heavy emphasis on Australian content'. Double J consequently garnered a reputation for not only eclectic playlists, but also radical talk content.

Comedy segments such as the sci-fi parody 'Chuck Chunder of the Space Patrol', Captain Goodvibes, 'Nude Radio' (presented by the stars of the cult TV comedy series The Aunty Jack Show, (with Grahame Bond, Rory O'Donoghue - and Garry McDonald), Fred Dagg (aka

John Clarke) and the station's legendary 'anti-ads' informed future program-makers on how humour could be used on radio.

Double J also featured regular news broadcasts, current affairs programs, political commentary by noted journalist Mungo MacCallum, and audio documentaries like the controversial *The Ins and Outs of Love* (produced by former 2SM producers Carl Tyson-Hall and Tony Poulsen), which included frank interviews with young people about their first experiences of sex. The Tyson-Hall and Poulsen documentary had allegedly 'breached community standards' and, although the ABC reportedly received few direct complaints about *The Ins and Outs of Love* (originally broadcast on Sunday, 23 February 1975). This documen-tary sparked a debate in the media and the Broadcasting Control Board reportedly asked for talks with the ABC.

Two days after the documentary was broadcast, the Fairfax tabloid *The Sun* published an editorial calling for the station to be closed, and a week later, the influential marketing/advertising industry journal *B&T* followed suit, demanding that the station should be forced to undertake one of three options: Double J should be closed down; the station's programming should be completely revamped; or the removal of those staff responsible for 'the present series of lapses'. Colleagues recall that Marius Webb was largely responsible for shielding the station from external criticism.

His career in the ABC forged ahead, and in 1975 he was not only elected to the ABC's Board as the Staff Elected Commissioner, but was eventually appointed to be the Head of Personnel (or as Marius put it, 'The Controller of Human Happiness').

Which brings me back to the Social History Unit (known in ABC jargon as SHU) and how it benefited from the death of the ABC's Radio Education Department which in 1975 was skating on thin ice. Once an important part of school curricula throughout Australia, the advent of television and other communications advances had meant that schoolchildren were no longer sitting in their classrooms listening to the ABC. The job of Director of the Radio Education Department came up in 1985, and a senior member of that department in Melbourne, Jenny Palmer, applied for the job. It was privately agreed that if she was successful, she would effectively preside over the abolition of this now redundant department. She won the job, and released both Daniel Connell (in Sydney) and Bill Bunbury (in Perth) to work for the fledgling *Social History Unit* (*SHU*). Most permanent jobs in the ABC are subject to appeal. A senior member of the Radio Education Department in Melbourne, John Patrick did appeal Jenny's promotion, and was successful. This was a disaster for Plan A to wind down the Radio Education Department. (Although this did eventually happen but much later than it should have been.)

Jenny Palmer was left in limbo, which is when I had a phone call from the Head of Personnel Marius Webb. 'The Controller of Human Happi-ness' told me about what had happened to Jenny, and asked me if I would take her in to the Social History Unit in Sydney.

'Take her in', I yelled into the mouthpiece, 'I can do better than that – she can fucking run it'!

I have to admit to being a lousy administrator. I often failed to take tedious Heads of Department meetings (which seemed to be called far too often) seriously, and made flippant remarks at inappropriate moments. In any case I got paid the same whether I made programs or was the Executive Producer of SHU. Making programs was what I really wanted to do.

So I welcomed Jenny in with open arms. Jenny and Ros got on very well, and Jenny let Ros act in the EP position from time including a period when Jenny took several months of long service leave. Ros took over as EP full time in 1991 when Jenny had to run an all-States training program in January 1992. For personal reasons Jenny went back to live in Adelaide where there was no ABC job for her, and Ros took over the running of the Social History Unit permanently. I had no problems with this. She ran me at home and at work, and was always firm but fair.

Indeed, in 1994 she sacked me! It happened like this. The powers that be wanted a reasonably high-profile redundancy in radio, and Ros put my name forward. I don't think she even bothered to tell me! But this was fine by me as there were lots of projects I wanted to work on outside the ABC including writing a history to mark the 50th Anniversary of the founding of ANARE (Australian National Antarctic Research Expeditions) now re-named The Australian Antarctic Division in 1947. I was 56 years old, and had worked for the ABC full time for 29 years and 11 months (didn't quite make it to 30).

But I am jumping ahead.

. . . .

In 1978 Ros and I decided to put our two boys in the deep-freeze for a month to have an overseas holiday. Well actually Ros' sister Julia said she would look after them. We had got to know Greg and Margaret Mortimer rather well. Greg was the first Australian to climb Mount Everest and just about every high mountain you could think of, even in Antarctica. Greg had also involved himself in Antarctic tourism by hiring ice-strengthened ships from the Soviet Union (which was going through a bad patch and could not afford to make full use of their own ice-breakers). Margaret specialised in organising land tours in exotic locations, and told us she was planning one that would begin in China, where we would drive to Xinxiang Province on the western border of China, and then drive over the Karakorum Mountains into Pakistan following the ancient route of the Silk Road, before flying back to Australia from Karachi. (A journey that would be impossible today, or at best extremely unwise.) The brutal persecution of the Muslim Uighurs by the Central Chinese Government was yet to occur in 1978.

Margaret was fascinated by Central Asia, but only two couples signed up for this excursion. It was unlikely Aurora Expeditions would make a profit with only two couples signed up, but Margaret decided to go ahead anyway. We met our travelling companions, Gerry and Wendy Commerford, for the first time at Sydney International Airport. They were inveterate travellers, and Ros and I were amazed at the amount of luggage Wendy had, but that was how she travelled and the ever-amiable Gerry was clearly accustomed to making sure it all stayed with them.

We flew to Bangkok in early September and then on to the highly polluted atmosphere of Beijing in China to be met by our guide Zxijin

Tim and Ros in Beijing's Tiananmen Square in 1998 beginning their journey from China through to Pakistan over the Karakorum Highway, following the route of the ancient Silk Road.

'The Fabulous Five' about to head off over the mountains to Pakistan. From left: Gerry Commerford, Wendy Commerford, our fearless leader Margaret Mortimer, Ros and Tim Bowden.

(his name more conveniently anglicised as Freeman) in the small Toyota coaster bus which would eventually take us over the Karakorum mountains to Pakistan. At dinner that night we found that as foreigners we were segregated from the locals and offered an entirely different menu, doubtless with enhanced prices to match. This became a pattern, unfortunately, for our few days in Beijing.

Our first excursion was to the Great Wall, and as we left Beijing and drove out into the countryside the few trees we saw were shedding their leaves revealed birds nests both large and small. Ros asked Freeman what birds had built them. Freeman's English was less than fluent, and he took a deep breath.

'In China we have three kinds of birds. Black birds, yellow birds and happy birds'. We conjectured that the lives of China's birds were unlikely to be very happy as the Chinese shot and killed just about everything that flew (or crawled) for the pot.

The Great Wall of China is actually part of a network of many walls built alarmingly over the tops of the mountains for some 5000 kilometres 2000 years ago to keep out unwanted invaders from the north. The restored section nearest to Beijing was more like a theme park, swarming with Chinese tourists who were intrigued by us few foreigners and lined up to have their photos taken with us. It was also a public holiday which probably explained the seething hordes of locals. Wendy noted in her diary that the general atmosphere seemed like Disneyland, complete with a Kentucky Fried Chicken outlet!

Wendy later wrote in her diary:

The Wall was a mixture of stairs and steep inclines. There were stalls along the way for drinks and medals and certificates for sale stating that you had walked the wall. One could even shoot an arrow off the wall with an archery bow. Below the wall you could get dressed in traditional costumes, sit on a horse or camel and have your photo taken. It was terribly hot and humid with the city smog still obscuring much of the scenery.

Next day we were taken to Tiananmen Square where only seven years before the military tanks had crushed and slaughtered the students who had been campaigning for more freedoms and democratic reforms that never came. Tiananmen Square is next to the Forbidden City built between 1406 and 1420, which is so large it would take at least three or four days to see properly.

We were ready to leave Beijing, with its choking pollution which made our eyes sore as well as the chaotic traffic mix of bicycles, donkey carts, cars and trucks which was so bad we wondered if we could get to the airport for our four-hour flight to Urumqi on time. Actually the four-hour flight to Urumqi was most pleasant, and we munched on packets of plump apricots and managed to glimpse glances of the widely dispersed Great Walls improbably built over the tops of mountains even through the enduring smog of Beijing.

Urumqi, the capital city of the Xinjiang Autonomous Area, seemed a smog-free paradise after Beijing, occupying about 1/6th of all China populated by fifteen million Uighur Moslems, with 1.3 million living in Urumqi. We were intrigued to see the men and small boys dressed in the same clothes, dark striped suits with long trousers, and cloth caps, looking for all the world like little old men. In the distance we could see some mountains capped with snow, a hint of what was to come.

Our new guide in Urumqi was Jing, a friend of Greg and Margaret Mortimer, whose English was excellent, unlike the struggling Freeman who had guided us from Beijing on our arrival in China. Our new driver was Ling who spoke little English but that didn't matter with Jing in control of communications.

On Thursday 1 October we set out on a two-hour drive to the well named Heaven Lake, through rich agricultural land with paddocks of cotton, sunflowers and winter wheat. Our cameras quickly swung into action when we stopped near a golden hill of corn cobs drying in the sun tended by a small family group.

Our next photo stop saw us invited into a circular canvas Yurt belonging to a Kazak nomad family.

Wendy's Diary Thursday 1 October:

A young girl, perhaps about 19 or 20 was left in charge of the 'mobile home' and animals. The floor was covered with rugs and all the bedding was neatly folded and stored at the rear of the yurt. We were offered hot buttered tea that was milky and tasted strongly of salt. Fresh bread had been baked in a small oven outside the yurt. Two men arrived by horseback and they also came inside for a hot drink. We sat in a semicircle with the young girl being the perfect hostess. I couldn't bring myself to eat the cheese that was matured on racks outside the yurt. The Uyghur men took off at breakneck speed on their horses.

Heaven Lake was picture-perfect despite the thousands of holidaying Chinese. We enjoyed a short boat ride on the lake. Tim and Ros had their photos taken by Chinese families – no doubt Tim's typically Australian wide-brimmed hat was a big hit.

Wendy pointed out a pregnant woman this morning – the first obviously pregnant woman seen during our time in China. The policy of one child per family was then enforced and contraceptive pills and abortions were free.

It was time for our last internal flight in China before tackling the Karakorum Highway from Kashgar. On our way to the airport we visited the Chinese Peoples' Museum.

Wendy's Diary Friday 2 October:

From the outside the building was a big grey block, but inside were absolute treasures. And enormous building with a lot of dust – the exhibits were labelled in Chinese (of course) that Jing was able to translate for us. Many of the ethnic groups had displays of their clothing, cooking utensils, goods and associated bits and pieces. This helped me to understand some of the people I had so far I met in China. An amazing display of five mummified bodies in a darkened room was really quite an experience to see. Some of the clothing was intact, hair still attached to the scalp, and footwear remained in place. The bodies were excellent condition due to the arid conditions in the desert where they were found near the town of Turpan. It was estimated that about 3800 years had passed since these people died. Despite the bodies being a valuable historical find, I always feel sad and want to cover them to give them some dignity. An impossible task. It is quite haunting in the way – peeking at them through a glass case wondering about their lives and loves – sadness overwhelmed me.

Our new guide Wang and driver Ling met us as Kashgar Airport. I had renamed our group *The Fabulous Five* and this stuck. With only five of us we were having a fabulous time and could be very flexible. As Wendy noted in her diary: 'We could stop when we wanted to take photographs, or tally longer to explore places of interest'.

The next day Wang arrived to take us out in the surrounding desert. But first we stopped in the outer suburb of Archuz. We looked at carpets and local craft but did not buy anything, rather discouraged by the overwhelming stench of human urine, before heading out into the desert towards the 7th Century town of Ha Noi, now in ruins.

Wendy's Diary Saturday 3 October

We all thought it was a good idea to visit – why not!? 10 minutes later, after trying to cross a ditch, we were hopelessly stuck in the sand. We all piled out of our small Toyota bus and discovered we had no recovery gear, no spare tyres and little water. After much forward efforts, reverse efforts, pushing and shoving, our guide Wang came to the fore. He chipped away at the compacted sand with a knife and after what seemed like hours managed to free the rear tyres. Our driver Jing 'gunned' the engine and the Toyota was freed more by good luck than good management. We agreed to forget our visit to Ha Noi.

As this was the bus we would be in when we tackled the remote Karakorum Highway it was not a reassuring outing.

Sunday was market day in Kashgar and we were due to begin the official start of our journey the following day over the Karakorum Highway on the old Silk Road Route over the mountains into Pakistan.

The current Karakorum Highway is the southern section of the ancient Silk Road, passing over the Khunjerab Pass 17,000 feet between the Pamir and Karakoram mountain ranges. It is the road link between China and Pakistan. For centuries this route was used by camel or donkey caravans negotiating the perilous Silk Road.

Khunjerab means 'the valley of blood', a reference to local bandits who took advantage of the terrain to plunder caravans and murder the merchants.

Nearly twenty years were required to plan, and level the present road between Islamabad and Kashgar. The highway is now a 1200 km road across the highest mountains in the world and one person died for every 1.6 km of road during its construction.

Lives were lost due to the blasting of mountains, rockfalls, unexpected avalanches and the odd earthquake. Some 40,000 people were employed or drafted to build the road.

The Karakoram Highways threads its way through the highest mountain ranges in the world – the Pamirs, the Karakorams, the Himalayas and the Hindu Kush. From Kashgar to Islamabad the Karakoram highway crosses the entire collision zone of the Asian Plate.

Five glaciers, over 50 km long are found along the roadside. Rockfalls, mud and floods are frequent and unpredictable. So much blasting has been done in the construction that the mountainsides were shattered and are still settling!

Would we have come if we'd known this in advance! Of course we would. Were we not 'The Fabulous Five'? At least it was autumn, and not the wet and unstable spring when more rock collapses on to the narrow mountain road were more likely. The road was officially opened in 1982. There are 25 major bridges and more than 70 minor ones.

A new road took us out of Kashgar (with special lanes for donkey carts) but the road soon turned to dirt as we started to climb through the Ghez canyon with steep mountains beside us, notorious for its rock and mud slides that often temporarily closed the Karakorum Highway. Wendy noted in her diary that we could actually see the far off high winds sweeping the snow from distant mountain peaks. We kept an eye out for signs of the original Silk Road and delighted in photographing the low stone walls that still marked the ancient stopping points.

We overnighted at Kara Kul Lake 3900m above sea level. Wendy was feeling nauseated, light-headed and had a headache through altitude sickness. An elderly Kyrgz man arrived with his donkey, dog, and a bactrian (two-humped) camel on which Margaret and I took turns to ride. An act of some courage by Margaret who hates both camels and high altitudes!

Wendy's Diary Monday 5 October

The small Kyrgz population produced some local craft for sale. Ros purchased a small beautifully hand-woven red rug. Gerry was badly affected by the altitude and was in no mood to bargain or buy. Back on the bus we made a 'hospital' bed on the back seat and made Gerry as comfortable as possible. His face was flushed and his sinuses were throbbing with pain. We were all concerned about him. Travelling at 3900 metres was a new experience for most of us.

Tashkurgan, which in Uyghur means 'stone fortress' was our overnight stop. Margaret had made it clear that the accommodation was very basic – but I must say I have stayed in a worse motel in Western Australia! Dinner was so-so and we were feeling so-so. In eight hours we had travelled from 800 metres above sea level to 5,000 metres. Perhaps this is why I managed to clean my teeth with a mouthful of vodka! Gerry was using our empty water bottles to smuggle alcohol into Pakistan. Gerry and Tim thought this was a terrible waste of good vodka.

Gerry and I certainly did, and found it difficult to understand why Wendy had seen fit to tip two large bottles of perfectly good vodka down the sink after her teeth cleaning shock.

Wendy's Diary Tuesday 6 October

Tashkurgan was importantly our exit point from China and we braced ourselves for formalities. We had to off-load all our luggage which then passed through an x-ray machine which no one seem to watch. Passports were presented and after much page turning were stamped. Illegal guns by gun-smugglers is a priority here and once they were sure we will clean we were allowed back to the bus – trundling our luggage behind us. A military officer then came out of the bus and checked our passports again – this was conducted in a very serious manner. All seem to be in order so we took off and drove about 100 metres when we were again stopped at the boom gate.

Once again we were checked – this was becoming frustrating – and allowed to exit China with a very formal salute.

Although we would not officially enter Pakistan until we reached the small town of Sost, we passed a lonely little hut near where we had lunch.

This checkpoint was particularly and pleasantly staffed by an amiable Pakistani who wandered along the road to talk to us. As Wendy noted in her diary, the main topic of conversation was not about our passports but about cricket! I had brought with me some gold Kangaroo lapel pins with me and the guard immediately pinned the one I gave him onto his lapel.

I recall this journey through the Khunjerab Pass at, 4,730 metres, as one of the most scary sections of our journey. The road surface had deteriorated badly, and our driver Ling now had to drive on the right now we had nominally reached Pakistan. The road was so narrow anyway I realised that if any oncoming traffic appeared we would have to move to the edge of the narrow road. It was just as well it was autumn, as the wet spring weather caused more landslips. As it was, it was unwise to look up, as huge boulders were precariously hanging over the so called 'highway'. Looking down was even more scary, as there was a sheer drop of some 1000 metres to a rushing milky-coloured river at the bottom of a valley. Of course there was no safety rail.

We were also conscious of the miserable condition of our Toyota bus, with four bald tyres and a spare that was in an even worse state if that were possible. Also our driver Ling seemed oddly preoccupied and driving more erratically than usual. Suddenly he pulled over (to the left fortunately) and stopped the bus.

Wang, our guide, cleared his throat and said: 'We have stopped because the driver has a problem'. Considering our precarious situation, not only in no-man's-land between China and Pakistan, the last thing we wanted was our driver to have a problem. It was, however, easily solved when Wang explained that Ling had to hide his local Maotai liquor bottles behind some rocks before we reached the official Pakistan border at Sost. He would collect them on their return journey.

Wendy's Diary

Sost sits at 3100 metres and has recently become the customs and immigration point for Pakistan on the Karakoram Highway. The small town reminded me of a 'truckies' pit-stop in Australia. This was our first chance to see the brightly coloured, highly decorated trucks used by Pakistani drivers. A tiny area is left free of decoration on the windscreen for the drivers to see the road ahead, and small bells are attached to the front of the truck, jangling as the truck bounces along.

We were met at the Sost customs and immigration depot by our new but very worried Pakistani guide Baig. It was now late afternoon and he had been waiting since 11 am. No mobile phones to check on our progress there! Pakistan is three hours behind China – actual time was really no great importance, we just made use of the daylight hours.

Margaret spoke for all of us as we were officially 'stamped' into Pakistan. I'm sure she had her fingers crossed behind her back when she declared that we were not bringing any alcohol into Pakistan! We were most careful to drink alcohol in private – our 'happy hour' at the end of the day, which became very furtive as we definitely did not want to offend our host countrymen.

The highlight of our descent from the border town of Sost into Pakistan, and eventually to the capital Karachi for our flight back to Australia was our visit to the fabled Hunza Valley.

Wendy's Diary Thursday 8 October

School lessons came to mind and a recent National Geographic article came alive. The Himalayan mountaineer Eric Shipton said the Hunza Valley was 'the ultimate manifestation of mountain grandeur'. The valley also inspired by James Hilton to write 'Lost Horizons' about Shangri-La,' the perfect place to live'.

Scientists have discovered that many 'Hunsakers' do enjoy a long life. There is almost no social stress and the staple diet of apricots and a low intake of animal fat are contributing factors. Many people are in their 100th year and still work in the fields. The drinking water is rich in minerals which looks like porridge and tastes like gravel. Apricots, grapes and mulberries were growing in any available corner. Apricot soup is a must for breakfast. No preservatives or spices are used – herbs being the flavouring agents.

The flat roofs of the small mudbrick homes are used extensively for the drying of produce which in turn produced wonderful mosaic patterns. Terraced gardens are watered by nations irrigation system flowing from the glacier in the surrounding mountains. Mt Rakaposhi (7790m) with its slender peak and the Karakoram's could be seen from our hotel.

Whilst we had been travelling in Muslim areas we were most particular to behave accordingly. The ladies wore loose clothing, covering as much of themselves as possible – we also wore hats most of the time. Jerry and Tim didn't wear shorts and didn't drink alcohol (in public that is!). We were mindful not to walk in front of a Muslim praying – this would have put us between the devout and Mecca. Displays of affection – touching or hugs – were permitted between males and females. It was considered okay for our guide Baig to help the ladies over a stone wall, but not our husbands.

We were now driving through areas that were anti-American. DOWN WITH THE USA had been painted on the larger boulders by the road workers. It was prudent to stay in our bus, as unfortunately we were often mistaken as 'Americanos'.

As we drove through small hamlets there were no women to be seen at all, just Pakistani men cradling rifles in their arms. The weather was becoming warmer as we descended from the mountains until we reached The Great Trunk Road which we hoped would eventually take us safely to the Pakistani capital Karachi.

Wendy's diary Monday 12 October

The Great Trunk Road was absolute bedlam. Think of any sort of vehicle – from large trucks to pathetically small donkeys pulling large loads, people dragging small carts – it was all on the Great Trunk Road. People also slept beside the road and sat in the middle of it with one lady actually feeding her baby as the traffic went past on either side of them. I wondered if one old man I saw lying beside the road could have been dead, but the people around him showed no concern. The road did not have any central lines marked and there seem to be no regard to the safety of anyone on – or beside the road. Children, some tiny toddlers, played beside this chaotic road. We followed trucks carrying cauliflowers to market, buses overflowing with people more than once 'admired' the rear end of water buffalos and cattle as they were driven, hopefully, to greener pastures. My diary notes stated, 'Busy, busy – chaos – confusion – noise'. The Great Trunk Road once ran 2500 km from

Kabul in Afghanistan to Calcutta in India. Rudyard Kipling once described as the 'broad smiling river of life'.

We were looking forward to getting to Karachi and our flight back to Australia. Overnighting at the Pearl Continental in Rawalpindi. While filling in our registration forms we noticed some young men who had to be Australians. They were dressed in shorts and sandals and looked familiar. We suddenly realised we were looking at the touring Australian cricket team on their way to a Test Match in Peshawar.

Our last day in Pakistan was in the capital Islamabad where I managed to be stricken with 'travellers' tummy' by stupidly eating a meat dish quietly festering its germs for me in the line of Bain-Maries, keeping the food within permanently luke warm as more was added from time to time. Ros, Wendy, Gerry and Margaret escaped by sticking to vegetarian food from the Bain-Maries.

We still faced a two-hour flight to Karachi, where we joined in with the locals praying to Allah for a save journey.

Wendy's diary Tuesday 13 October

Karachi airport was unbelievably terrible. We had a five-hour stopover and had to collect our luggage. It was reassuring to know that our suitcases were accounted for but the trick was to get them, and us, onto the next floor where the departure lounges were. All the lifts were locked and after some confusion we hired a porter to take our luggage upstairs. The Mafia controls the airport and that makes it impossible for people to transport their own gear – hence you have to hire a porter. We arranged and paid for Margaret Ros and Tim to join us in the club lounge. All was well for a few hours and then we were hassled, by the staff, for more money. This was about 1 am and we were the only people in the Club Lounge.

I wanted to (foolishly) get the police until I realise they would most likely be corrupt too. Gerry went back down to the check-in counter to try and clarify the situation to no avail. It was really most unpleasant and the young men were doing their best to intimidate us.

We were at a stalemate until Ros told them forcefully to 'fuck off' (with all the charm and grace of her middle-class background) and we were then left alone, still wondering if we would ever see our luggage again!

We flew out of Karachi at 3 am on Thai Airlines via Bangkok and Jakarta for Sydney.

It had been a wonderful journey, and as Wendy put it, 'We had enjoyed each other's company and not once had there been a problem or any unhappiness between us. The group dynamics were perfect'. And not the last of our journeys with those indefatigable travellers Wendy and Gerry, with whom we sailed to Antarctica some years later.

Fabulously decorated Pakistani trucks.

5

Ros' Books

In the course of Ros' distinguished career as a maker of radio documentaries, she wrote three books published by the ABC. All are now out of print.

Ros' first book was *Aspects of Nutrition* first published in 1986 after the broadcast of her series of documentaries on food drawing on the expertise of nutritionists, allergists, herbalists, naturopaths and other knowledgeable 'foodies'. 'You are what you eat' is a quote that has been traced back to one Anthelme Brillat-Savarin, in 1826 in his book *The Physiology of Taste.* He actually said, 'Tell me what you eat and I will tell you what you are'. This implies that if you eat what is considered to be healthy you *will* be healthy, and if you eat what is considered unhealthy this will make you unhealthy, which is drawing a long bow.

In her Foreword on *Aspects of Nutrition* Ros wrote: 'Australians are very fortunate to have such an abundance and variety of food available to them. Although some families cannot be confident that they will eat the next day, the numbers are comparatively few and increasing range of ingredients seems only to lead most people further away from the most important reason for eating… to keep the body healthy.

'When we were considering topics for *Aspects of Nutrition* we chose subjects and experts most likely to stimulate thought and discussion. Some, perhaps a little controversial, would not find a place in a traditional school of nutrition, but in the light of new ideas now being expressed they do have a place in the re-examination of our eating habits. They also encourage us to think about the food we eat as an exercise in nutrition I'm not simply as a way of pleasing the palate. None of the nutritionists I spoke to was against delicious or tempting meals, but most advocated a return to the natural flavour of individual foods rather than a cooking style that masks taste by mixing natural ingredients with a number of complex flavours.

'The maintenance of health is a very compelling argument for a more thoughtful and educated attitude to food. Medical treatment and sickness benefits cost the government millions of dollars every year, not to mention the economic and personal toll on individuals. This cost can be reduced drastically if people take responsibility for their own health and know how food, exercise and other factors such as stress can affect their well-being.

'In modern society, with its ephasis on technological solutions, we often wait for a complex and highly expensive operation to cure a medical condition rather than take an operation to cure a medical condition rather than take responsibility for our health in the interests of prevention.

'*Aspects of Nutrition* is by no means a comprehensive survey of the latest ideas of nutritional science – in fact, listeners have suggested enough topics for another series. What it does is question some popular beliefs about eating habits and suggest ways of achieving along, energetic and healthy life through a more discriminating approach to food. The choice lies not with the community, the doctor, all the government, but with each individual.'

• • • •

What is a healthy diet?

'Technology is so clever, our knowledge is so great, that you can take a lump of almost anything, converted it texturally, change its colour and flavour, give it a name and serve it at the meal table. It may have no relation to any known food whatsoever'.

Xandria Williams

Our lives are so governed by sophisticated technology that it is often difficult to think about ourselves as a part of the animal kingdom which, like birds and beasts, has evolved over thousands of years and adapted to the environment. Only a few decades ago, people living in remote areas could lead a simple life somewhat similar to that of their ancestors several hundred years before, but this is no longer possible. People living in even the most isolated settlements in this country are now able technically to watch a sporting contest while it is actually being played in another continent. Intellectually we can comprehend this and adapt to it but we tend to expect the same sort of 'speed-of light adjustment' from our gastrintestinal tract, a system that takes just a little longer to change.

Xandria Williams is a biochemical nutritionist and naturopathist where who's background is in chemistry and who has clinics in the Sydney suburbs of Beacon Hill and Cremorne. She writes for the health magazine Australian Wellbeing, *is working currently on a book on allergies and is head of the Nutrition Department at the NSW College of Natural therapies.*

A commonly held idea in nutrition today is that if you eat foods from the four basic food groups – namely flesh fruit and vegetables, cereals, and dairy products – you will have a well-balanced diet.

It is interesting to look back on man's history and ask if this really could have any evolutionary basis as a true statement. What you find is that of a modern nutritionist had asked any of our ancestors over the last million and a half years about their diet they would've failed the good nutrition test because I only ate food from two of those basic groups. As far as we can establish they would have eaten a diet moderately rich in flesh – we have this image of man as a hunter gatherer, but he was probably a scavenger and a gatherer, eating game that other animals would have killed, and if he had lived near oceans or rivers he would have eaten fish – and the other part of his diet would have been fruit and vegetables and occasionally seeds. It is most unlikely the primitive man would have had any dairy products at all there's very few wild animals would have stood still long enough to be milked! It is also unlikely that he had any greens or seeds in quantity as modern grains with a relatively compact seed head have only been a feature of the world in the last 10,000 years or so – not very long in evolutionary terms but by evolutionary standards a balanced diet would be one with somewhere between 20 and 50% flesh, 50 and 80% fruit and vegetables and no dairy products or greens at all. However, we have adapted somewhat, I'm in the jeans have changed, over the last 10,000 years or so – not very long in evolutionary terms.

By evolutionary standards our balanced diet would be one with somewhere between twenty and fifty per cent flesh, fifty and eighty per cent fruit and vegetables and no dairy products of grains at all. However, we have adapted somewhat, I mean our genes have changed, over the last ten thousand years to the diets we have now, and we do include in the so-called 'balanced diet' the dairy products and the grains. But, even so some of these foods are among the very common allergens and a lot of people are unable to eat them, and that is an interesting thought to consider.

It is difficult in modern times to assess who would be eating a balanced diet. If you live in a city you have been eating food that has been picked some time ago. It is not as fresh as it used to be, as it has been growing on the same ground over and over, crop after crop, year after year, and the ground has become depleted. We put superphosphates back but we do not put the nutrients back.

Nobody eats food as it grows, everybody eats processed food of some sort. So we are not getting a diet as rich in nutrients as diet from which we evolved and which, presumably, by the excepted evolutionary way of thinking, is the sort of diet a man should aim for.

David Phillips has a doctorate in Nutritional Science, is in demand as a lecturer and broadcaster in the field of nutrition, runs a practice in Sydney and is the best selling author. He has some suggestions for a healthy dietary regime.

Seventy-five per cent of the diet should be comprised of succulent foods: fresh foods and vegetables. That is man's natural dietary intake. The other twenty-five per cent can be concentrates which are generally in one of three major areas – proteins, carbohydrates or fats. The major sources of natural protein are nuts, seeds, whole grains and sprouts followed by beans and lentils. If you want to go further, there are the dairy products – eggs and cheese, but not milk. Milk is not a protein that man can assimilate because he has no enzyme called rennin in the stomach after the teeth are properly formed to break down milk.

Nutritionists have no doubt about the validity of the saying, 'You are what you eat' because health and well-being are inextricably tied up with food. The analogy about running a high-performance car on low octane petrol is often quoted, but that only covers foods that could have more nutritional value. There are other foods that are actually harmful. In his book

book Your Life-style, Health and Nutrition, *Russell Frank Atkinson has coined the term 'illth' foods.*

There are 'illth' foods and healthy foods. A health food in my opinion is a whole food, you eat the lot. 'Illth' foods are the ones which are fractionalised and which are grossly out of proportion to what one would expect in nature. You cannot get a spoonful of pure sucrose in nature, you can only get that from your sugar bowl. You cannot get completely denatured carbohydrates from nature, you only get them in white bread, for example, so that these things have to go if we are interested in good nutrition. The term 'illth' is an attempt on my part to classify the foods that really have no nutritional value at all, very little.

In order of 'illth' I would put the more or less plastic foods at number one. Unfortunately these are the ones that so many children eat. Television advertising between 4 pm and 6 pm is full of inducements to eat things like ice blocks. There is no food value in an ice block. Then there is junk food, which comes very close after, a lot of foods, not just confectionery, which are in the same category. Junk foods are things which have been highly processed like fishfingers and some of the cereals switcher allegedly good for you, the breakfast cereals, for instance, where the grain is completely fractionalised, has gone through extensive processing, has other chemicals with it and can be loaded with sugar. I classify some foods junk food because they are situated with fat, fats. It is been estimated that in the United States – and we follow them very closely – it is possible to obtain forty per cent of the daily calories in fat. Now that is weird, it has never happened before in the history of the world.

There are other 'illth' foods that are more or less fifty-fifty; well not too bad but they are not too good either. These are foods such as tea and coffee which do have some food value but which are easy to overdo because they tend to be a bit addictive.

Foods in the next category are takers and givers. They hand out a lot up front but kick you in the tail. Alcohol is one of those. It seems to give you energy and pep you up but in fact at robs the body of some very important micronutrients. Zinc and magnesium are eliminated in the urine if you drink a lot of alcohol and you chew up a lot of the B group vitamins, particularly vitamin B1. There are a whole lot of foods like that which we take daily, which can appear to have an advantage but which then kick you in the tail.

Some of these foods are good foods which have been compromised by our storage methods or growing methods. Unfortunately, the cosmetic effect of a shiny apple impressed the sellers at one stage, so they coated their apples with paraffin to keep that shiny look. Paraffin not only seals in any toxic insecticide which may be on the skin, so you cannot get it off, but if you eat a lot of apples and like the skin (where the nutrients lie) you would tend to hold in your intestine and not absorb the oil soluble vitamins – A, E, K and B. I am not saying that if you ate a lot of apples you would run into a deficiency syndrome but the apple is not doing you much good. It is only a matter of finding out about these things and reading the material (because the material is there) and plotting lifestyle to compensate.

Another problem is not just a lack of micro nutrients in the food, it is the soil and growing methods. It is possible to produce splendid looking vegetables which are big and fat and juicy which are in fact severely lacking in nutrients.

(Author's Note: Here ends some sections of Ros' first book on Aspects of Nutrition.*)*

BEING ABORIGINAL

In the 1970s and early 1980s and even 90s very few radio documentaries or documentary films were being made about First Nations people, and those that were made tended to be made by interested white journalists, broadcasters and film makers. Today that would be unthinkable as Aboriginal people have well and truly taken over their own ancient and modern history as custodians of this land and do not need white Australians to be involved.

But when Ros Bowden's book on her documentaries *Being Aboriginal* was published in 1990 it was breaking new ground.

'I first came across aboriginal people when I was on a six months drive around Australia. Like most travellers I found my first images distressing. The outback seemed to have groups of dusty drunks on every pub veranda, often accompanied by sounds of shrill arguments sprinkled monotonously with those famous Anglo-Saxon four-letter words.

'The white people in the town explained it all away by suggesting that colour produced all this hopelessness, that black people were somehow naturally dim-witted and therefore could not manage their lives. Criticising these people for being drunk and hopeless while there were many equally badly behaved whites inside the pub did not provide any of the answers. Because I had spent a good deal of my childhood in South India and Sri Lanka where black people managed their lives perfectly adequately, I felt colour in itself could not explain things. Curiosity developed and I tried to understand what had led to the scene outside the pubs.

'My reward has been constant challenges to my own perceptions. Almost every contact I have with Aboriginal people forces me to rethink the way I am conditioned to understand things. Accepted standards of cleanliness, the work ethic Europeans are all bought up with, our selfishness in capital accumulation for the benefit of only of our close family, these all look pretty illogical when examined from a different angle. The road to the pub still stretches ahead.

'Recording material for the ABC Social History series *Being Aboriginal* was part of this discovery process. I had contact with a variety of Aboriginal communities. The group involved with Yipirinya School in Alice Springs were language speakers with a good part of their traditional culture woven into their lives. The people taken from their Aboriginal parents and "raised to think white" were trying to make contact with their wider family and birthplace. This knowledge was their passport to acceptance in Aboriginal society. At CAAMA Radio in Alice Springs, American country and western songs were the vehicle for the characteristically Aboriginal custom of keeping in contact with relations living hundreds of miles away in the desert. Why not their own songs. I naïvely asked?' 'Because' I was told,' Aboriginal songs sometimes take six months to sing'!

Many of the reasons for the scene outside the pub are now obvious to me. The solutions are less so. But as I listened to the customs and values of Aboriginal people explained to me so patiently and generously by all the groups I met, it made me wonder how long the white community can go on pretending not to hear and continuing to keep Aboriginal Australians waiting for justice.

A number of people were involved in each of my 'Being Aboriginal' programs but in this book we have not attempted to identify each speaker separately.

RAISED TO THINK WHITE

(Those taking part in Chapter One, 'Raised To Think White' are, Coral, Lola, Joy, Robyn, Cherie, and Kevin.)

I was taken from my mother, my mother was taken from her mother, I have my daughter was taken from me. Link-up isn't only about taking people home physically. Really, what Link-up is about is getting people home emotionally and every way so that one day they can stand and say, 'I'm worth something as an Aboriginal and as a person.

Nearly all aboriginal families in Australia today will know of relatives who were moved as children and put into European care. They are the children the Aborigines referred to as 'Taken'. Their place in their family is vacant but never abolished. Many of these people, now adults, are suffering a crisis of identity and want to re-join their own people. But they have been 'raised to think white'. To be accepted in Aboriginal society they need to learn a completely different set of rules.

Coral Edwards, coordinator of Link-up, experienced all the difficulties herself when she went home to meet her Aboriginal family.

'*Link-up*' started in 1980 with Peter Read and myself. It started because I went home to meet my family and it was after that when we got back, I thought, "Jeez, it's taken me this long to get home there must be a lot of people around who are in the same boat", and that's when I put it to Peter. How about we start something for people in my position, like me? And that was how *Link-up* started.

'We were rather naive at the time, thinking it would be so easy to start. We thought we only work with adults who had gone through Cootamundra or Kinsella Homes and we had no funding and had no idea where we would get funding. We had no idea about the welfare system or where you found records or anything.

But in spite of difficulties linkup was established and people came for advice and help.

'My mother was Aboriginal. The policy was to separate children, especially fair skinned children, from their mothers as soon as possible. On my certificate of removal it said, "Take the child from the association of aborigines as she's a fair skinned child". 'I think the rationale behind that was to raise me as white.'

. . . .

'I was adopted when I was, I think, about 20 weeks old to a white family in Sydney and that's where I grew up. They were a middle-class family and I grew up with one younger brother. We grew up on the northern beaches of Sydney so it was a very middle-class suburb and there were no other Aboriginal people around that I knew of.'

. . . .

'I know for a fact that I was adopted when I was only a couple of months old. When I was younger I didn't want to have anything to do with the Aborigines. I sort of thought of myself as being a white person. In fact, if ever I heard the word Aborigine I'd back away, so to speak, but that was when I was much younger, and then as I grew older and wiser I came to terms with it.'

. . . .

'I remember very vividly Central Railway Station as being a lot of activity going on. There was a Welfare Officer, a male Welfare Officer, there was myself, my younger sister and my older sister and my brother. The male Welfare Officer was there to take my brother to the boys' home and I remember him crying to stay with us and the Welfare Officer dragging him away. That's been very vivid in my mind and I haven't forgotten. You know, that was quite a number of years ago, in 1951, when I was only four, and I don't have a memory as to why we were taken away. My next memory is of the Matron in the Home. I was told to go out back and wait for the other girls in the Home to come back from their walk. After that it's sort of dawned on me, "Well, where's Mum? She wasn't around any more.'

. . . .

'For quite a few years I grew up thinking I was an orphan, because all the other children used to have either one of their parents come in on visiting day, which was the first Saturday of every month – I'll never forget that – and I used to have no one so I sort of thought I was an orphan. Then I found out I had a mother. They also told me she was an alcoholic, she drank a lot, that she didn't want me and I have nowhere to go, but if I kept on playing up I would be sent to Cootamundra Girls Home which was only for bad girls. I was running away, stealing. It came to a point where I had shot through overnight and they took me up to the doctor to see if I was still a virgin, which I was, and then I was told the next day that I was Aboriginal and that I had mud in my veins and that my mother didn't want me – all in one day and then I had to write out, I think it was 500 times, God is love.'

Coral Edwards says she does a lot of talking and a lot of listening to people who come to her.

'Listening more than talking – to find out how they're feeling about themselves and how they feel about Aboriginals and what sort of misconceptions they've got, so we can help them. A lot of Aboriginal people who come to us have been raised with a non-Aboriginal family and the only information they've got about Aboriginals is what they've got off the TV or the radio, which isn't always good – it's not a good image. So we do a lot of listening with them and a lot of crying with them. It's often the first time people have actually told things that they've never ever said before in their lives about things that have happened to them. It's a sort of unburdening, if you like, to get rid of stuff and start afresh before they go on to the next step, which is meeting the family.'

. . . .

'Mum, my foster mother, used to say things like, "Oh I'll take you to Redfern one day and will show you what your mother would've looked like". They'd say things like, "She'll be sitting in the gutter drinking a flagon of wine", and all this sort of thing and when you're a kid that's really scary. You get drummed into that kind of thinking that Aboriginal people are dirty and just wasted – that's the sort of ideas they put in you. When I went through school I just couldn't adapt really well to the other children because I was the only dark-coloured girl in the whole school. That's all I knew – I'm Aboriginal and I'm darker than anyone else, that's it.'

. . . .

'Comments were made – little things like, "Oh she'll be going walkabout soon" – stereotyped comments, as I used to wonder what the hell they were all about. I used to stand a certain way of the kitchen sink and didn't realise that I was standing in what is now a stereotyped Koori position. They'd come along and kick my knee so I'd fall and break dishes, so I'd have to go and write another thousand lines of a Bible verse – I was a great one for Bible verses. But I just grew up with the feeling that being Aboriginal was bad.

. . . .

'If I had been fairer it may have been a little easier – I don't know, but I felt like I was in limbo, like I wasn't one side of the fence or the other, but I was just stuck in the middle somewhere. We were constantly told to keep clean – "you don't want to be dirty like the Aboriginals you see around". We were being raised to think white and act white and forget about anything that was Aboriginal.'

. . . .

'When I found out that I was Aboriginal, one of the biggest things that I had to start doing was looking really closely at all the things I learned and the stereotypes, I had to look at things like being taught by white people – I don't just mean by that my family. I mean the school that I went to and the newspapers and just everything around me – the white culture that I grew up in. I had to start questioning all the things I learned through growing up like that. I felt really frightened that I'd take all those judgements home with me and put them on my family, because they're wrong and an absolutely bad place to start from in trying to get to know your family. It's hard enough getting to know strangers anyway, let alone putting all these judgements and rubbish on them.

. . . .

'I was 36 when I started to think that I was black, in my mind, because I have been working and living in white society for so many years. I've been discovering my Aboriginality since 1983 and there's no way that I will again ever think white.'

. . . .

'It took along time to get over that thing of black not being a colour of your skin. I've been told to believe that to be black you have to have really dark skin. That's partly also why, growing up, it was harder for me to identify as Aboriginal, see myself as Aboriginal, because I thought that I didn't look Aboriginal enough to be Aboriginal. And all those things like, "You're so fair you can't be Aboriginal", and -

"What about the part of you that isn't Aboriginal", and, "What percentage of you is Aboriginal"? – All those questions were what I'd grown up with around me so it is actually quite a long process feeling that I could comfortably identify as black.'

. . . .

'How many times have I heard said, how can you really consider yourself an Aboriginal person when you had a white father, or if you've got white blood in you? You cop it all the time from white Australians, and I just say to them, look you are what you are and I am what I am. I'm an Aboriginal person. What are you? "I'm an Australian", they say. But what are they, really? What are white Australians? They're always questioning our identity and we always have to prove our Aboriginality, but when have white Australians ever proved their identity?'

. . . .

Coral Edward says it's hard to explain the need to find out about being Aboriginal.

'It just drives you. It takes over your whole life. Do you want to belong so much and you've got no base to start on, because if you start mixing with Aboriginal people the first thing they going to say is, "What's your name and where do you come from"? And if you can't answer those two questions then you're gone. People can't connect you into the Aboriginal network because they don't know the name, or you don't know the name, so they sort of shut the door straightaway. That's why it's really important for us to get to know what the natural name is, because as soon as we've got that name we can pack pick the area. For instance, my family name is Edwards and there are only three places in New South Wales where there are Edwards families. We talk about our country, our spot … Aboriginal families didn't move far from those areas. People say, Edwards – where are you from? Are you from Burke or from Balranald or Tingha? And I say, "I'm a Tingha Edwards", and people just click you in because they know. One of the most common Aboriginal names probably would be Williams. Now, there are Williams not connected with each other, different Williams families from the North Coast, South Coast, out West, and Smith is another one and Johnson is another – we know Johnsons only come from certain areas. And so that's why it's really important for people to have that name so we can just click them in.

'If someone came to us and said their name is Williams, for instance, we would contact those areas and not just ring up. We don't ring up, we actually drive to the town and go and see the people, because it's just the right thing to do, and find an older person who remember. And the thing is with children being taken, people remember that. It's not something that's just forgotten, like yesterday's birthday party. They say, "Oh, yes, so-and-so had a child taken, you know, 30 years ago", or something like that, and she's married to, say, someone else now, but she wasn't Williams. People remember. You just don't forget something like a child being taken.

'People contact us through word-of-mouth. They ring through or write letters. A lot of welfare agencies – Aboriginal child care agencies, Youth & Community, in fact any government offices, in fact any inquiries at all, they just put them on to us.

'I found out I was Aboriginal when I was 25 through a fairly long process of firstly walking into the Aboriginal Legal Service in Redfern and to see Jenny Munro and saying, "I think I'm Aboriginal. Can you help me"? And she did. She was great. She spent quite a few hours with me, talking and just making me feel that it was quite likely that I'm Aboriginal and that was a good thing to be.

'Then she wrote to Coral and Link-Up and they traced my mother, who was a white woman and to tell them that my father is Aboriginal. Because I was adopted that all took about 18 months.'

. . . .

'I wanted something fast, something that you could feel really quickly and there wasn't anything around. It seemed like such an effort.

'I was working at Newtown Social security office when I found out about *Link-Up* and I rang up and talked to Coral and she had a talk to me about what to expect and that she'd do her best. I think it was only about three months after that that she found my mother's name, and that for me was the biggest breakthrough.'

. . . .

'We were just talking, just sitting there having a yarn, and Coral says, "Your mother's not Dora"? I said, "Yes", and she said, "You know there's a lot of people looking for you". I said "Oh, yeah, pigs might fly – who'd be bothered looking for me"? And she said, there's a whole lot of people in Cowra and they're all your cousins and your auntie's, and she said, "Yes, it's where your grandmother's buried". That was marvellous, although it was very scary, too. Then Coral said, "Well, look, I'll take you home", and I liked the way she said "Home". I was sort of thinking of a nest somewhere, and even then it took me weeks to decide whether I would go home or not. And that was horrendous. Oh, my God, I'll never forget it! You know, we were getting closer and closer to Cowria, tearing along the highway in a bloody white Commodore which reminded me of a Welfare car, when I said to Coral, "Hey, come on, let me out here. You go on up to Cowra. The motel's already booked, so you go up and have a nice time I'll just take a walk back to Nowra. No trouble, no trouble, I'll just go back. Bye-bye". Coral said, "Listen Joy, "we will go on to Cowra and book into the motel. If you don't want to go over to meet Val and your cousins you don't have to". We got to the motel, unpacked everything and then she said, "No we've got to go and meet Val". And we drove up, but I was just sort of super-glued to the car seat and I started balling my eyes out, and we went in and there was a whole lot of faces and names – I'm still learning names. And then she introduced me to Val and Val was just beautiful, just beautiful. She just said, "G'day love". She said, "My grandmother and your grandmother was sisters. And I just flew to her. You know, we started crying and carrying on and, oh, it was marvellous. That was the first time I felt I *knew* who I was. It was like going into the womb and coming out born when I met Val, and it's been like that ever since, sort of growing up inside. Because inside I've got this family vacuum. I can't say, "Oh when I was ten I did this with my cousin or I did that with my mother", but all that vacuum now is starting to be filled and it's quite schizophrenic at times, too, because you've got this child growing up inside you and the *adult* you has to learn to let that child grow and it's very difficult.

. . . .

'In a lot of people there's a strong girl feeling of wanting to belong somewhere. That's not in all people though it tends grow in all of them, but at the initial meeting it's usually a curiosity to find out who you are, get your family history, and the rest follows after that, stronger feelings of belonging somewhere, and all the Aboriginal thing comes in as well.'

. . . .

'With relationships there are certain things in the Aboriginal society that you just don't do, and I'm learning those – what to do and what not to do. You can refuse a biscuit or a piece of bread or a slice of cake or something, but you never refuse a cup of tea. There are people that you go and see first, not a pecking order, but there are people you go and see first and people you spend a certain amount of time with. There are some that you can talk to about certain things and others who can talk about other things.'

. . . .

'Aboriginal families also extended – that's the biggest thing I think, getting used to having heaps of people in the house, cousins, aunties, uncles. There might be ten living under the same roof. There might be a lot of them living on benefits. Some of them don't. A lot of them work sometime. Always if you've got money and your brother hasn't and he needs money to go down to the shop and get something, well you just give him money and you'll give everyone money. If they need something they're very unmaterialistic. Money isn't an issue. It's surviving, you know, and we've all got to survive, so you give it away so everyone can survive.'

. . . .

'I was put through the hoops a couple of times. I made one horrendous mistake when I went back by myself the second time Jane's fridge was empty. So big magnanimous me, I decided to go out and do a whole lot of shopping and spent about $80 to $90 on groceries and filled up the fridge. That was in the morning. In the late afternoon nearly all the food was gone as I said, "Jane, look, all those bloody kids are running around eating this food that I bought for you. There's only one loaf of bread left". Then

I open the fridge and I went through everything that was left, I knew the fridge had been full, and she said to me, "Listen here, little woman, you didn't buy all that food just for me, you bought it for all of us. Once one of us is got the food, we all have the food. Those children out there are just as hungry as my children are in this house, so", she said, "Don't come up here with your high-falutin ideas of thinking you're doing me a favour, otherwise you can just piss off now". That was the most marvellous thing she ever said to me because if she could talk to me like that it showed me she really cared and she wanted me to learn how things were done, not how to *be* but how to *show* I'm Koori'.

. . . .

In the white culture not to look someone in the eye all the time that they're talking to you is rude; it's like you're not paying attention. But to look Aboriginal people in the eye the whole time you're talking to them is rude; because you're staring at them. That was really hard to get used to. It takes a long time to accept that something you learned as good manners in one culture is wrong in another, a long time to be able to do that and feel comfortable about doing it. It's like being in a no-mans-land in a way, because you don't know Aboriginal ways enough to feel comfortable and to know that you don't sort of stick out as someone who doesn't know quite what they're doing half the time. You're trying to watch other people and trying not to make mistakes and laugh at the wrong things... your whole body language is different. I'm sure I stick out like a sore thumb to people and they wonder, they think, this woman is a bit strange. Also I found out that I lost a lot of contact with the white people I've spent a lot of time with. That was a long process, partly because they didn't understand why it was so important to me to find out where I was from and also because it became an absolute obsession that I just had to know everything that was to do with who I was. And because most of the white people I knew didn't really understand it, I lost a lot of contact with them. You're a bit in limbo for a long time I think.'

. . . .

'There's a natural bond that I feel towards Aboriginal people that when I was thinking white was never there. I've rediscovered that. You'll just nod, even if you don't know them, if you see them somewhere, in a restaurant or in a pub, or walking down the street. It's "Cous",or "Sis", or "Brother". You just do it.'

. . . .

Aboriginal people are getting a lot stronger. They're feeling like their own people. They're uniting more. And they're doing it again and they're doing it a lot to rejuvenate the culture, just bring it to people's eyes. Once people know about where they come from – their country, their tribes – and they've met their families, then they've got it inside, and they know little bit about traditional society and how traditional people lived: That's all they need.'

. . . .

'I want to say that I feel I'm regaining my Aboriginality. To me at the moment it means that I know where I'm from, I know who my people are, I'm starting to know who all my relations are and to meet them and get to know them as my aunts and uncles and cousins and my grandfather. I'm learning very slowly the history of the area that I'm from and it is a sense of belonging, and unless you feel that you d*on't* belong it's really hard to explain how important it is and how precious it is knowing where I'm from.'

'When we got to Arambi Mission I was told to stand and look all around, which I did, and they said "Now, all of that's yours". It's all bounded by natural boundaries. None of it, before the *gubs* (white people) got here anyway, none of it was subdivided for individual use.

'This is part of the land rights question we never *had* sub-divided for individual ownership: that territory was bounded by natural boundaries.'

. . . .

'I had to know the history, to know where I came from and to be really knowledgeable. There are a lot of Aboriginal people that wouldn't know what I know, although they know it in a different way than I do. A lot that

I know is from books, but they know it because they've lived it or their father or grandfather lived it and it's been passed down that way.

'I have to know things because when you get with Aboriginal people they talk about the old times a lot and you like to be able to participate, too. It's good to sit there and listen and learn; it's also good if you know a little bit, even if it is from a book.'

. . . .

'As an Aboriginal person it will give me something to identify myself by to know that I do have a family. When I'm with other fellow Aboriginals I feel a certain bond, a certain magic. I feel like I'm part of the family. It's a wonderful feeling, actually a feeling of joy, a feeling of pride. Para Aboriginal Letty means to me that you come from the land. It's your land, Australia, the trees, the grass, the seas, the deserts, the rainforests, are all linked with yourself. It's something nobody can take away from you.

6

'White Man Say We Have No History'

(In Chapter Two, of Being Aboriginal, *White Man Say We Have No History* features Essey Coffee, Les Darcy, Marlene Lord, Richard Sullivan and archival recordings of Jimmy Barker from the Australian Institute of Aboriginal Studies.)

'We didn't have any history according to the white man. We are one of the poor old races that didn't have anything in writing so it's only hearsay. If you put it in writing it's history.

'There's so many young people who ask, what will be like? Over our mothers and fathers? What were our tribal names? What was the link in our tribes? I'd like to see our young people learn their traditional ways again so they could put a value on their own people instead of having to value the European value of life.'

'Brewarrina is a small country town in the north of New South Wales. To Europeans, that's all it is. But Aborigines have a history in the area going back 5000 years. It was one of the biggest of the tribal meeting places on the east of the continent. Intricately constructed stone fish traps provided food for thousands of tribal people. They gathered there for ceremonies and to renew contact with relatives. Present day Aborigines are planning a cultural centre overlooking the ancient fish traps to record the history of the people. It will also inform other aborigines and Europeans about the rich cultural heritage of the area.'

'The museum was my idea in the first place. It's my dream story and it was all created by me and a friend of mine and we decided we are trying to recreate Aboriginal culture in the north-west of New South Wales. Our theme was the Dreamtime stories of the people. When the land was a desert there was no water and no river. *Baiame* the creator, came up the river, making it. Digging the river, his spirit dogs made the Paroo, other spirit dogs went up the Warrego, he came here, and each place he went to he was helping people as he formed the river. When he came to Brewarrina he made the rocks, told them how to catch fish by making the fish traps, and on leaving Brewarrina he left his footprints on the rock, which are still there today – an enormous thing 20 feet by 30 feet. And so that was the theme of our museum – that we create the Dreamtime stories to make something that will make everyone aware of their traditions and make people proud of being Aborigines again.

The river flows swiftly when there's been rain. That water covers the Aboriginal fish traps that have existed for an estimated 5000 years. Some of them are now destroyed. The rocks were used to make causeways and crossings in the 1880s when paddleboats went up the Darling River.

It's interesting to reflect that all the time in that 5000 years up until very recently there would've been Aboriginal families camped around the area, sure of being able to catch their dinner in the fish traps that had been built by their ancestors. Those fish traps now are not in use but they are still a very important part of the cultural heritage of the Aboriginal people of Brewarrina.

'Dreamtime is as long as we have been there and how long that is I don't know but we'd have to say thousands of years. You'd have 500 yards and 100 yards across the water and that's the size of the traps. They were made out of stones running across the river like sheep yards in a way and you'd have the catching pens you'd hunt your fish into and then you'd get them into one yard and close it off, you'd hunt them into another yard where the water was shallow, and then you would gradually get them into water you could go and spear them or *nullah* them or knock them out some other way. Apparently they were owned by the Ngemba tribe and they would invite you here – when I say 'invite you', I mean invite other tribes when the fish were plentiful. There are records of what I'm saying – that there were four or five thousand Aborigines at one time in Brewarrina when the fish were running. They would come here for the ceremonies and get together and enjoy their traditions of meeting and playing and having fun, like they do today – swap yarns and talk and get to know relations and meet again after they've been walking around for the year or years or whatever time.

'The yards, the traps were actually there, it didn't need any knowledge or anything to set them up. There are the outlines of the original traps. I can remember some old men talking about the old fishery and that's where some of the biggest corrobories were, on the riverbank.

'The old people would meet there. But a tribe couldn't come across another tribes' boundaries unless they were invited to do so. All that's part of the old people. Did meet up from the fishery and invite the other tribes to come down – tribes from the Culgoa and further beyond Burke and Enngonia and those places. It was a very special place in the lives of the old people. I'd love to see it done up again. If the old traps were there it would always remind you of the old times, the old people.

. . . .

'Once we knew a lot of stories. There are a lot of tribal Aborigines who knew good stories, mythical stories, if you like, that were told to us. But even our people after a while disbelieved these tribal people. No doubt a lot of the stories were mythical but they were very good and had a lot of good meaning to them. The old chap that told me one particular story was Mullacky Barnes who was our uncle, our old tribal uncle and a wonderful old aboriginal. His wife Dolly – she was a lovely old woman – died. The legend used to go like this: There was "the time to go home" voice. It was a mythical voice, and when again where this voice sung out "time to go home" was at a place called the *mirrigunnah. Mirri* means dog in Ngemba and *gunnah* means waterhole. And out of this waterhole came Merioola, the spirit dog. Of course we never ever heard this voice – "time to go home". It was a mythical voice and as this Merioola came our of the *mirrgunnah* – this was the waterhole – the Merioola was the size of, say, a domestic cat, but as it climbed up the bank it grew in size until it was the size of a Shetland pony and it disappeared. It didn't matter where we were in the bush with these people, just before sundown this voice would sing out, "time to go home', this mythical voice. And when the sun got to tree top level in the west we'd get a premonition, if that's the word. Somebody would say, "time to go home'. And if we were eight or ten miles from the Mission we'd be gone, back to the camp. And I was told by my old uncle this was a message to keep the kids out of danger after dark, and it was a disciplinary thing, if you like, that all the kids were back at camp before sundown. And told me that when the whites first came into this part of the country there were dozens of cases of white kids being drowned and lost in bush country. And all my years as a young boy I never knew of one case of an Aboriginal child being lost on that part of the Mission or being drowned. That might have been a frightening story to some of the kids, but it was a very good way to keep them out of danger so that was one mythical story that I knew, and there were others like that.'

. . . .

'My father originally came down from the Warrego area – that's Queensland. He came down, and his two brothers, Ben and Alfie, and his sister Ruth. They're real name was Goodgebah– their tribal name – because they were tribal people. When they came down to Cunamulla, old Arthur Shillingsworth adopted them – three brothers and a sister – and put them in his name. That's how my people came to be Shillingsworth today. One of the biggest tribal places was Dungowan. There were many tribes there at the time when my father met my mother. She was a Bailey. He married her but then the police – troopers – sent the trucks out to round up all Aboriginals and put them in one place on the Mission. They took them all from Dungowan. My mother and my father took off – ran away – and they couldn't find them. They even had policeman – you know, troopers on horseback. They rounded the rest up and took them to Angledoole. That was the next big Mission to Dungowan. They brought in everybody from everywhere, Kamilaroi, Eurelaroi – all the Aboriginal people, even from Tipooburra. They took all the Aboriginal people and put them in one big yard in Brewarrina and made them live there. They sent everyone to the Mission – all the different tribes – and they couldn't lead their own life. They tried to make them walk about in white people's clothes – tin buttons on their shirts and braces on the trousers and things like that. They used to come along and split up the different tribes.'

. . . .

'The original aboriginal tribal area was in Brewarrina itself at the fisheries. There were the two tribes the Morowori and the Ngemba. The Aborigines weren't mugs even in the tribal days. They knew where the high country was, and the flooded areas, and so Brewarrina was the spot these people lived it. When the settlers came into those areas they were automatically pushed off that higher ground there. And of course they were shifted out miles upstream from Brewarrina to a settlement called the Mission.

. . . .

'There was afree issue of government rations – what we called three-eight-and-a quarter. That was eight pounds of flour, three pounds of sugar and a quarter pound of tea. We'd line up with a little roll-out bags and a few milk tins and get our rations. There was a free issue of tobacco – plug tobacco – for the older people, and the fine-cut packets for the younger men that smoked.

. . . .

'In those times there was plenty of rabbits there and every afternoon me and the boys, all of us young fellas would go up what we called the "hard bank" and we camp out of a night. We'd go up there in the sandy banks to what they called the retreat. Ww'd go up there to get rabbits and that – we'd knock 'em with a stick. And there were plenty of fish then, at the time. We'd camp out there on the river bank and set our lines of a night time and sit back there all night and hunt again the next morning before coming home.'

. . . .

'The native fish which were there in large schools at the time were easily caught. We used to have a natural weed that grew from the edge of the water out on both sides something like eight to ten feet. So at different times of the year, especially in the winter months when the fish would stop running, there was always a source of food that we could harvest, if you like, from the weeds around about. One method that we used was to get a forked stick, a big stick and put it down in the weeds and twist the stick around and, of course there would be three or four of us onto the stick, and we would pull the weeds out and in turn turn you'd pull out beautiful big shrimps and blue crayfish and small native fish that only grew follow about six to eight inches at full growth. When they would come out – and they'd be a dozen of us along the river pulling these out for the older people –that be a source of food there all day for us. So that was another source of food that we used to get there on the old river.'

. . . .

'We used to go out a lot as kids, not so much with the men, we used to go out with the old women, and they used to have what they called a *gooli*. Some of them still had the skins they'd made inti *goolis* but the government blankets, the free issue blankets that we used to get, were turned into *goolies*. They used to just chuck them over the back of their shoulders, and of course, they'd carry a lot of stuff in there. If they were small kids around some of them bounced up into the *goolis* and the women would carry them around like that. But they were great gatherers of food. The women did all those sort of things.'

. . . .

'I was taken away when I was eight years old and I didn't come back until I was about 17.

'I can just remember getting in the car – the Welfare man put me in the car, and was taking me away and Mum was there waving and I was crying for her. And I couldn't go back because they were taking us away. I still don't know today why they took us away. Two sisters went before me, and then I went and then the smallest one went and we all ended up in the same place, Cootamundra.'

. . . .

'There were quite a few kids taken in the later years, you know, around the late 1950s. Poor old Hilda had three children take an off her from the Mission and sent to Cootamundra and another old lady there had two boys taken. I think there was remorse and sorrow here for the children that were taken. People didn't like it, but those were the laws in those days, and the boss, the manager, had the full say in everything. If he said they have to go, well, that was it.'

. . . .

'She didn't talk about it much when we came back. She was just glad to see us, I think. She said she used to go up to the station all the time and see if we were there, but we weren't. When I came back I didn't even know where to go. I thought they were still at the Mission. This woman asked me where I was going and "I said I'm going out to the Mission to see my mother", and she asked me, and I told her, and she said, "Oh I'll take you down". And we just got off the train and Mum came running out crying, when she saw me.'

. . . .

'The police were always there to enforce the law even up till I was 15. We used to live just over here and police came around, you had no say in anything, they were the law and they could walk into your place and we were bought up to be scared of them.'

. . . .

'I believe the New South Wales Police Force was equipped with Harley Davidson motorcycles at the time in the mid-1930s they used to have a motorbike with a sidecar on Brewarrina, and it used to have the Sergeant in another constable and another guy driving. Two used to come to the Mission get each one would have a rifle – I think it might have been a repeater .22 or pump action rifle. If there were any dogs there in the street tthey'd be automatically shot. But we were a wake-up to the police coming out. We'd put a leash on the dogs and away we would go into the timber with them and we'd hide there until the police went. We had to do that because it was our only way of getting meat – emus and kangaroos. It was impossible to run them down by foot so the only way that we could get them was with the kangaroo dogs, we used to call them. They were a source of getting food, if you like, for a lot of people there on the Mission.'

. . . .

'We used to make a *boondi*. It was a stick and it was about two feet long, a very streamlined shape, a thin handle, and it was well balanced and it was a throwing stick. When the rabbits were in millions in that part of the country we became very skilled with these particular sticks and you'd start a rabbit up out of a squat, a squat being a roly-poly (a weed ball) and three or four guys would get around this rabbit and start him up and he'd come out, bounce out, and you'd anticipate his move, of course. You'd judge his distance and then you throw two or three feet in front of him and you'd get him every time. So I'd say that our tribal people were very, very skilled with these particular sticks. You'd knock the goannas that live there off the trees, too, with them. We used to have a small marsupial animals there. We had the *bilby* in that area 40 years ago but they're gone now. He was a little kangaroo animal, long years, something like a hare, but he was very good eating.'

. . . .

'I learnt from men some of them in their sixtys and seventies to make this particular weapons that I make now. If you joined in the workshop – the workshop I'm talking about then was out on the wood heap – all I had was the a tomahawk and rasp file, and if you toed the mark and sat down there with these people and wanted to learn to make something, you were free to do so. You could pick up a stick and work it and they'd teach you what to do. But if there is anybody playing up they'd whisk them right out of it. We weren't allowed even to call them by their first names. It always had to be "Uncle".'

. . . .

'There were quite a few old fellers out there, I can remember, but we couldn't go near them – we have to walk past them, we couldn't walk in front of them or anything like that. We have to walk at the back, we couldn't put a shadow on them or anything. They were pretty strict with the young people.'

. . . .

'There were a lot of corroborees there. We used to help paint the people up, even though we were fair skinned aborigines. I don't know how we looked with the tribal people painted up and whatever, but we used to get in there and do the dances with them, as boys. They used to mix the ochre with the gum and the later years they used to get hobby glue and mix it with the ochre – that gave it it's sticky substance, I suppose. We had all sorts of colours – there about seven or eight different colours of ochres. One particular mineral we used to call *dohra.* We used to get it off the bank of the river and it would be chucked in the hot fires, pulled out and of course it was crushed up and mixed with water and it made a very good white paint. Even though our culture was gone then, there was a lot of incentive from those older people that used to have the corroborees there on different animals and whatever. And of course, when they were a couple of emus killed and brought back to the Mission and they'd be cooked and everybody would get a feed there'd be a corroboree that night and they were perform dances based on our day's hunting and they were very good.'

. . . .

'I loved going out there, especially walking around the old graveyard and down the old bend there where were used to fish. But now all those things are gone, and all the old people. But it brings back memories when I do go out there. Before, we rode all over here and hunted, in there... the places where the old people met. To me it's where I was bought up and where I'd love to spend the rest of my life.'

. . . .

'We've got our culture, we've still got her old ways of living. We might live in a white man's home home but we still have our black way, an Aboriginal way, because we live our life. My tribe is Morowori, my father's tribe, and I take after my father, because my father's name is Muri Goodgebah and that means a flower or a tree. This is my land. We own this land, as Aboriginals. We were first here, before Captain Cook came. This is my land here, where I look. We own all this, every little bush, every little tree, every log, every stick, every flower. You see those big flowers? Emus are getting fat now and getting ready to lay. We tell by the flowers because they're getting near spring time. This is our land. This not your land.'

7

'Language is Our Lifeblood'

(In Chapter Three, 'Language Is Our Lifeblood', are Freda Glynn, Ned Hargraves, Vince Forrester, Agnes Young, Isaac Yama, Emily Hayes and members of the CAAMA staff in Alice Springs.)

'When I first heard CAAMA and I heard somebody, I think it was Kenny Madden, read the news, I thought to myself, that's my language. Now I want to hear more being said, being read... I'm really proud of it, because it's my language that's being read to make us understand and to know more what's going on.'

'CAAMA (The Central Australian Aboriginal Media Association) has been broadcasting in Aboriginal languages to the people of Central Australia since 1984. For many in remote settlements it is the only information they get from the outside world. Although there is a danger that broadcasting major languages will smother the lesser used ones and cause them to disappear more quickly, there is no doubt that hearing your own language on radio and television contributes to a sense of identity and pride.

. . . .

'We started off with the three major languages and we seem to be able to cover from Tennant Creek Down to the Great Australian Bight because Pitjatjantjara is fairly large, Arrente is one of the largest Aboriginal languages in Australia and Warlpiri is a very distinct language group. But we're doing the dialects of Arrente, which is the country that we are broadcasting in, we are broadcasting Amatchera and because we are broadcasting to the country of the Kaidija people at Allekurung we also broadcast in Kaididja as well. We need to do Allywarra, which is another dialect of Arrente, and we are hoping to do Warrumunga, which we're broadcasting in Tennant Creek.

'There has been criticism about using major languages like Arrente,Warlpiri and Pitjatjantjara at the expense of the smaller languages. The people who study language feel that the other languages will get swallowed up if we maintain these big languages all the time.'

Ros: So there is a policy to try and diversify as much as possible?

'Certainly and what's been happening is that people doing the traditional stories – The oral history that we are collecting – speak in their own language, so they are being broadcast quite regularly. English may sometimes be the third or fourth language for some people around here – most people speak three or four dialects. We find that we can put three completely different languages on. We've got good broadcasters who can understand other languages and they can joke and laugh in two different languages.'

. . . .

'When I heard that these other languages we're going on air, I said, "Why not try my language? I asked if I could come down here to do the Kaidija show. I didn't really know how to speak Kaidija properly. I had to go back to Barrow Creek and stay for a fortnight on Neutral Junction Station – that's the station we were bought up at. I picked up all my languages again and now I can speak properly, I think. The old people back at Newtlands and at Barrow Creek like to hear me talking in Kaidija. The older people down at the camp all have wirelesses is now, so they just wait for when I start talking and they turn all their wireless is on just to hear what I've got to say for them. I think it is important for the Kaidija to go on because the other kids growing up like to speak it, I suppose, and the old people like them to carry on talking their own lingo.'

. . . .

'I do, CAAMA news in Warlpiri and also in English sometimes, but mainly in Warlpiri – everything I read in the paper is interpreted in Warlpiri. When we do these things they listen to it; it's good that somebody who speaks that language can tell them what's going on around the world. First, without, CAAMA they didn't know what was being said in English; only a few could understand it – those who have been in schools.'

. . . .

Ros: A lot of the programs are request programs and a lot of the requests are European songs, aren't they?

'Yes, it's very hard to explain to non-Aboriginal people that Aboriginal music is not suitable for broadcast, it's not a three-minute song. An Aboriginal song can go on for six months if it's done correctly. Say the migration tracks of the birds – they're sung over right the way from the desert to the coast of the Gulf of Carpentaria and back again. And while that migration period might take six months, people are singing those birds across all the time as they're moving. Each family takes it up as the birds migrate wherever they are. If they're here in Alice Springs the families here are doing it. If you go up a bit further to Bushy Park, other families are responsible for it and they keep singing the songs and they're different all the way along. It goes right up to Boroloola and the birds come back, circle back and return to the desert to lay their eggs again. So that story can be six months long. And it's really hard to take a three minute snitch out of songs that go on and on and on. If it was sung for Alice Springs it may go for three days. The songs are sung for three days with no sleep. People just sit there and sing as the birds go over. There is one story that is called the Atuthura Story and it goes from the desert here to the Gulf of Carpentaria. The stories and songs are both together, you have to learn the songs which are part of the story.'

Ros: If you're trying to describe your traditional stories, is it possible to tell them in English or can you only tell them in your own language?

'When there is something very difficult, a very hard word, sometimes we have to find a very similar word that can fit in that traditional word or corroboree or whatever that thing is. It's very hard and it's one of the things that Yabba people always worried about – putting similar things really close to something that's really hard for them to try to explain or show.'

'If there is something that I have to show – for example the designs for a traditional painting – I would use language, a bit of the language, but if it's not for white people it would be very hard for me to try and explain or try to make them see the picture or understand the picture. It's very hard for a European bloke to get what the picture is saying or what the picture is telling; it's very hard. English sometimes doesn't have the right word, and English sometimes doesn't fit into some of our traditional designs.'

. . . .

'Children who don't know the language, who don't know how to speak, how to tell stories, should try to get someone to teach them how these things are said and what the stories mean.'

. . . .

Ros: How important is language in preserving the culture?

'Oh it's our life blood. This is what we tell the young people. You have to know your language because you'll never be able to learn you're Dreaming and if you don't know you're Dreaming you can't identify where you belong. If you don't identify where you belong you may as well say you're dead. As an Aboriginal person you have to know your language to be able to learn your Dreamings.'

. . . .

Ros: Is English a very inadequate sort of tool to describe Aboriginal Dreamings and lifestyles and things like that?

'I think so, because I think that the word dreaming in English is sleeping – you know, sleeping what you dream about. But for us it's got nothing to do with that whatsoever. Dreaming is the tracks that you are responsible for. You grow up, then you have to maintain it spiritually. You've got to maintain it through not over-using it; you've got to do the ceremony is for the different animals; you've got to do ceremonies for human beings; and as you grow and as you get older you learn your responsibilities to that area. As you get older still and as you marry into different families, you take on the responsibility of other people, and as your children have children you take on the responsibilities of other Dreamings – their Dreamings, the children's Dreamings, which might go a different way from yours. It just depends who you marry. And it's all really very interesting and fascinating.'

. . . .

Ros: But the term Dreaming in English almost means lying back and doing nothing, whereas you're talking about a very active process.

'Yes very busy and you never stop learning. The Aboriginal currency in the traditional way was knowledge. The more Dreamings a person knew or the more tracks he had become responsible for, the more powerful that person became all the more knowledgeable that person became. And you never stopped learning. If you were the person looking after that track all that Dreaming, you were the one that was looked after. People fed you and you became responsible for the stories for that land and knowing all of things about that land and knowing the secret, sacred ceremonies for that land. The more you knew, the more you got looked after wherever you went because when the right time came for you to teach, you were then looked after by the people who you were responsible for.'

. . . .

'A long time ago people would all meet up and there was some areas that had their corroborees... to do with our cultural stories and this type of thing. So we've got to look at the political aspects of things because, of course, those gatherings were for political purposes, between tribes or between family groups. Now we look at how we send a message out to the community. I know if it's my language being spoken I will listen to that quite closely. But English...you can hear English and you don't really take notice of it. But when you hear your own language and what's being spoken in your own language, you do take a lot more notice. Since we've had CAAMA, the people are more aware of what politics is about because we can interpret exactly what the people are saying and we can let the community know what people are saying.'

. . . .

'Most of the Aboriginal Community here at semi-literate or illiterate. We've had communication skills since the beginning of time here and our communication skills are by word of mouth also the visual thing... like most of the news here in the Northern Territory, because the Aboriginal community is a large part of the population most of the news is on Aboriginal issues. We can get these news items and press statements and all this type of thing out to the communities in their languages with proper, skilled interpreters that can relay the message to the community.

'If a member of the ruling government says something on Aboriginal issues, that gets interpreted and goes out. If people say, from the ALP put out a message, that also goes out and the importance is that the community in the outlying areas know what's going on in the major towns such as Alice Springs, Katherine, Tennant Creek and Darwin. They've got information directly out to them in a language they can understand. So the language broadcasting here at CAAMA is one of the most important parts of our role in self-determination – the survival of the language whether it be Pitjatjantara or Warlpiri or Amadgera or Kaikija or Luritja. Because we use those languages up here in the Central Australian region every day, it helps self-esteem within the community: we have our own language, we can identify with our own relatives, extended family groups and things like that. That plays a major important part in the community. We can conversed in in about three of four Aboriginal languages before we can converse in English. There might be an Arrente bloke sitting down and listening to Walpiri news and he'll understand it, or a Kaidija woman sitting listening to Luritja news. You know, it's direct communication to the old men and old women of the country and we tell them what's going on there.'

. . . .

'I'm a member of the aboriginal community here in Alice Springs and I have been here most of my life and with that too Direction we've had a "Beat the grog campaign" going on. Well being a member of the community who has a high-profile in the community, I go around and I look at things such as shops and grog outlet places. But now people are buying more tucker than they used to before, more blankets, more clothes. Just through the communication of an anti-grog publicity campaign – "Why drink so much"? – the people are not drinking so much and that in itself has proved to me personally that it's happening.

'In our land rights issues we come on this wireless here and we can talk: we talk about what they are going to be doing in Canberra, about our land rights act. We went from Alice Springs with 400 people representing the tribe – that was through information going from this little wireless station out to the communities in the languages explaining what was going on. The people being involved knew what the amendments and changes were. The community knows about what is going on now, the community knows next time that their vote is going to be worth a lot more than it was previously because we are aware of the issues.'

. . . .

'From the outside it appears that we are just a request station – you know, people writing in – but that's part of being Aboriginal, letting everybody know where you are and who you are and whose family you belong to and all that sort of thing. But as people see the strength of the station and what it can do by having the language and by our young people being able to listen to their own language, it's a lesson in itself. It says, my language is important. Whereas, before, kids were saying, "It's not important; we won't be able to get anywhere with our own language; now we've got the opportunity to hear our own language, it's not being pushed aside".'

Ros: What sort of response do you get from those people on outlying stations to hear their own language over the airwaves?

'When we first broadcast, I've seen women cry when they heard their language on the radio, they were just so excited, laughing and joking. I don't think people could manage now without having CAAMA, without having a radio station that broadcasts their own language.'

. . . .

8

Learning Two Ways

(Those taking part in Chapter Eight, 'Learning Two Ways', are Eli Rabuntja, Theresa Alice, Rosie Ferber, Margaret Heffernan, Louise Raggert, Thomas Severns, Anna Norma Rice and Diane Ferber.)

It's important that the children learn their own language because it is *their own language. Why teach English to Aboriginal kids if they've got their own language?*

Yipirina School was the first independent Aboriginal school in Australia. It is in Alice Springs and its intention is to teach Aboriginal culture to Aboriginal children, thereby encouraging children to keep their culture strong.

The Literature Development Unit at the school makes books for the children to learn from. Dreamtime stories and contemporary oral history related by the elders living in and around Alice Springs provide the raw material.

'The first thing the Aboriginal council does is make decisions about Bush trips. There are a couple of builders who go out on bush trips, and camping out sometimes. They tell stories about the land and everything that came in the Dreamtime that the children should still learn. We take pictures, photos, and make videos, then bring them back to the school and work out how to make the books. We make a recording, too, and keep it in a file in the Literacy Centres, so that when we start working on books we can just take out the things we want to write about to teach the children in school. The stories that we write from the tapes will become lessons later to make books.'

. . . .

'We check the story out with the person who told it to the children to make sure that everything is all right to be written down, and then we start writing it. We also check with the linguists working here, just to make sure. In the old days people never wrote any Dreamtime stories all the stories that the old people tell us. we just heard what they told us.'

. . .

'It's important that the children learn their own language because it *is* their own language. Why teach English to Aboriginal kids if they've got their own language? They should learn and be taught in their own language so they can learn more quickly and it's their first language. It makes it strong with themselves. They'll be fluent then to speak and to write it. They can have anything if they know the language, make a book of their own or film, make a video… especially in teaching their own kids, generation after generation.'

. . . .

The Aboriginal Council were emphatic the control of Yipirina should not rest with them and not with the Government Education Department. The five year fight for registration which gave access to funding included an appeal to the Supreme Court. In September 1983 Yipirina officially became the first independent Aboriginal School.

'You know, we had big trouble before. Sometimes we would send the kids down the path and say, you have to go to school, not play around the street or down the creek there. Some of the white kids used to say, "Hey this is not an Aboriginal school. It's for whites". The kids were ashamed then and didn't want to go to school. At the government school they didn't help Aboriginal people.

'When I sent the kids in the morning to school and they got money for lunch, the white kids always took the money away from them. They went straight home, they weren't happy with that school. The white kids were cheeky all the time, took their money and hit them. That's why the kids always ran away. They didn't learn anything, Aboriginal or anything. White people's way was all they learnt at that school.

'At Yipirina school they are learning two ways. They speak fluent Arrente and that's why we have an Aboriginal teacher to teach them so they can understand. The kids come every day and I'm happy and the kids are very happy.'

. . . .

Eli Rabunja is an Arrente and the Foundation President of the School Council.

'The Education Minister asked me, "Hey, Eli, why did you start this Aboriginal school? You should go through the government school". I said, "I think this way. I've got to ask the Aboriginal people what they going to do with their kids, give them a government education or put them in the school. I've got to ask them first". "Well, that's all right", the Minister said, "Where are you going to get the money"? I said, "We are going to ask the government for the money".' There was trouble all the time before we were registered at Yipirina. Every fortnight government people came from Darwin, Canberra, all the Education people. After five years we were registered. Now we can't leave the school. We started it, and will just keep going with the kids, teaching'.

. . . .

'When I first came to work at Yipirina the school wasn't registered yet and at the time we were fighting for registration. It's gone a long way from when I first came to work here. It's improving every year, I think. There's about three languages being taught at the school now.'

. . . .

'It's important for the kids to go to the bush and learn everything about taking witchitty grubs, collecting all the bush food and the bush honeys.

'II was living in the bush a long time with my grandmother, and I'm teaching my kids the same as my grandmother told me, all the stories, the bush things and camping out and finding bush food and meat.

. . . .

The children are taught about the various medicinal qualities of the gum tree. They break off the branches and the outside bark to have a look at the sap and see the colour of things. They're being taught what these things can be used for. It's all part of being educated as an Aboriginal at Yipirinya school.

Just north of Alice Springs in a little bit of roadside bush the kids bang pieces of bark with a couple of stones to crumble it up and then put it in billy cans. Another group of kids make a fire. The idea is to boil the bark in some water and then use the liquid for sores – sore eyes and sores on feet and legs.

The mixture boils for 10 or 15 minutes, then it is left in the wind to cool for a while. The kids dip cloth or tissues into the mixture and wash their legs with it. Activities like applying the liniment to people's sores and cooking witchetty grubs are filmed for use in a classroom later on.

'I'm writing those stories about bush medicine and trees and plants for Yipirinya on my tape in my language. After, I'll write it in English and make a book for kids to read, Yipirinya kids.

. . . .

Eli Rabunja: Education means everything… that's why you've got to learn. We just take the kids to the bush first and show them food and water, where you go to find them, and take them around. That's education for Aboriginal people. In our culture there is a lot to teach the children about their own ways – there's both Western and the Aboriginal ways foot. But by education in European ways, we are mean schooling and stuff like that – jobs, how to survive.

'Today they think in two ways. It's got to be like that. We have two people here – white and black. Aboriginal people can learn something from what cultures and white people can learn from Aboriginal cultures. They've got to be learned together.'

. . . .

'My tribe is Arrente. My grandfathers are all around today and my kids are all Arrente.

'Alice Springs is really Mparntwe which means the Dreaming of the caterpillar. There's three different kinds of caterpillar but the Yipirinya is the main caterpillar here in Alice Springs. The story of caterpillars seems to be one of the histories of Alice Springs. Another caterpillar came from

Western Australia and the third came from the North and they joined into Yipirinya. They started to discuss around looking for food, then they travelled on to Emily Gap. Hills and trees here represent Yipirinya, like, for instance, these coolibah trees where they've built the water resource. That's caterpillar dreaming. They would travel aand all these hills represent the Yipirinya and the caterpillar. That's their track and they travelled east to Emily Gap where they found a home. It's a place where nobody can go, not even the initiated men. It's a special place, it's Amekameke.

'At Emily Gapget up you can see paintings that represent all three caterpillars. I usually take the kids around Yipirinya and I tell them the story of the caterpillar so they can keep it always and it can't be lost. It's still important. It can't be wasted away, it's got to be there always and passed on from generation to generation.

'We still look after Emily Gap and we get a good bit of help and support from the National Parks and Wildlife and Conservation Commission. They help us support and look after it. If that was destroyed, many of our elders would be dead and gone. There'd be a lot of sicknesses and you'd see many of our people dying away. It's where our strengths are kept. Once our important places are left untouched we will all be okay. The children understand this. I usually pass it onto them and we keep it as a record at Yipirinya school. So when I'm dead and gone the story and the history of Yipirinya will be there always.'

. . . .

'There's oral history being told by our old people, the elders, about the first white man, and I've actually got that from my father and it's been written in the book. We try and encourage the old people to tell us what happened in the past and they've got lots of stories to tell. They didn't really know what it was when they first saw a white person. They thought he was covered in some sort of paint or web, cobwebs. They said, "It's got two legs and looks like us, but the colour's wrong. Some were frightened but they hid behind the trees and had a look. They just saw this white man going past and they were actually living up the North Road – a place called Berts Plain – where my father used to live and my grandfathers. That's the first time they saw a white man.

'It was the explorer Stuart. He came past through Orange Creek and went onto Jay Creek and then came into Alice Springs and on to the old Telegraph station. He met other old people there and he travelled up north and that's when he saw my family sitting down and they said, "Oh, whatever is this? A spirit or whatever"? And he just went past and talked a little but they couldn't understand what he was saying.

'Some people who lived in Central Australia used to go down south visiting relations, and from time to time my family used to hear there were white people down south but they didn't actually see them, so for some of them it might have been a frightening site, the first time seeing a white person.

'You only read in white history books about white explorers and first transports and so on. You never hear about Aboriginal people. That is why we trying to get all the stories down in a book so the children can read about what happened before to our people.

9

The Spirit Of Musgrave Park

(Featuring the voices of Paddy Jerome, Bob Weatherall, Sam Watson, Don Davidson, Headley Johnson, Pat Murdoch and Roy Hopkins.)

'This is my perception of Musgrave Park – as an unspoiled segment of a once great spiritual piece of land that has been spiritual to a large number of tribes from the specific area of Australia... it is also a haven for me, where I can be an Aborigine without stress, without being ridiculed by Europeans and being looked down on as sub-human by Europeans.'

Musgrave Park is the square piece of grassy land the size of two, perhaps three, city blocks among factories and run-down cottages in South Brisbane. There's the usual toilet block in one corner. The streets bordering it are fairly heavily trafficked and there are even parking meters down one side. But there are some trees, big shady trees that are nice to sit under, even on a rainy day when they give shelter from the rain. There's a rough kind of football ground in the middle and cricket pitch in one corner. Altogether it's a fairly typical inner-city park.

During the Commonwealth Games in 1982 thousands of Aboriginal people from all states gathered in Musgrave Park to attract international attention to Aboriginal rights. The protests were peaceful and successful. and the park became the focus for the black struggle in Queensland.

'It was really a magical feeling having Aboriginal people coming from all around Australia. We had people from Tasmania, the Northern Territory and Western Australia – and all other parts of Australia, even from our community reserves. A tent city was established. It was quite a big tent city; it had marquees and things like that for people to and people also slept in cars, and were put up in hostels and church buildings. We took people into our own private homes as well because there were a lot of elderly people and we didn't want them being subject to police harassment at that time, or the white harassment that was around. There's only one particular area of the park that was used all the time, which is the closest park to the Brisbane River. The other area was used mainly for sport or some kind of cultural event, and we all met and stayed within the one area. Everybody lived there, sharing, contributing to how the struggle would be fought at that time, how we were going to get our messages across. It was a great landmark for Brisbane, and a great landmark for Australia, and you had thousands of Aboriginal people really working together and putting ideas together. It was just brilliant, I think, to see everybody there together.'

From the Commonwealth games experience came a desire to protect Musgrave Park from development and make sure it's remind an open space where Aboriginal people could meet for celebrations, funerals or to make decisions that affected the whole community. To ensure the area for future generations, the Aborigines had to document the ritual and social significance of the park. It was planned that the information would then be made into an educational kit to illustrate the importance of the park to Aboriginals, and also to add weight to requests for Aboriginal control of the area in the future. The Foundation of Aboriginal and Islander Research and Action received a research grant for the project from the Australian Government. They went to written sources, and to the Archives. But first they tapped oral memories – like these – of the Aboriginals living in Brisbane.

'I was taken to Musgrave Park by Uncle William McKenzie. I think he was 94 or 96 years of age at that time. He came and he said, "Look, this is Musgrave Park, this is a tribal ground", and he sat down and told me and Pastor Don Brady and a lot of elders in that time the history behind that certain bit in Musgrave Park. The initiations of the people took place there. Women came there to conceive, the battles between the different tribes were settled here, the talks were there, sitting down for peace or fighting. All the disputes with settled there. But there are a lot of things that I can't tell you, which are very sacred to me. If I did I'd be persecuted by my own people – not by the people living here but the people who are dead and gone now. It is an unwritten law that you can only say so much. But that was my first introduction to Musgrave Park by Uncle

Willy McKenzie. Although I knew Musgrave Park had existed for many years I did not know the true meaning of it.'

. . . .

'Musgrave Park has been a gathering for my people, Aboriginal people, since the beginning of time. I know that all different tribes right throughout South Queensland have been coming to this area long before any white man or European. They've come from as far as Gympie, as far south as Southport, and as far west as Toowoomba – a lot of different tribes to the one area living peacefully at the same time. The Woolloongabba area was actually the place where they'd meet on the battlefield and sort out their differences. When someone was seriously hurt then that was more or less the end of the fight and there wasn't a total annihilation of each tribe. We lived pretty peacefully together really.'

. . . .

'These people would gather over here every four years for festivals. My tribe would participate by allocating certain areas of the Bunya Mountains for specific tribal foraging. But if someone transgressed on someone's area, the issue was settled by feets of strength or show of arms or whatever, in a controlled environment. And we do have our corroborees, our initiations. Where Brisbane now stands was the overall area where the allocations of the land by my people were held, and the actual ceremonies of the land allocation were made on Mount Clutha'

. . . .

'Oral history is the most significant history from the Aboriginal people because the park has been developed in some way, and a lot of evidence has been removed from the area. But the oral history that the Aboriginal people still maintain is that a *bora* ring existed, that there are three graves of Aboriginal people within the area, and that the path to Vulture Street runs back into the Woolloongabba where you'll find another *bora* ring.

The history of the area, the vegetation that grew there, what Aboriginal people ate, what they used – animals and plants and those type of things – have been revealed as well.'

. . . .

'There is an abundance of evidence showing that Aboriginal people have a significant claim to make – historical and social – within the area. Written information is available in John Steel's book on Aboriginal pathways that surround the South East Queensland area, and other written records, and it stands beside the information that the Aboriginal people have been talking about'.

. . . .

'We're doing all this research, and it's making people aware. Not all Aboriginals are aware that there are six burial grounds in Brisbane that we know of, and there are probably 100 sacred sites or *bora* rings. Certainly white people don't know anything about it. We're going to use this information to make people aware, but also although Aboriginal people can't claim land in Queensland, if it came to a claim, we've got evidence which could stand up in a court room. Musgrave is the heart of land rights, add aboriginals are the original owners of this country, but we're not recognised as such.'

. . . .

'We'll fight in any way to retain that park. But let me make this one important point: we are only on this earth for a short time, and from there will go to Hell or Heaven. That's what the white men say in the Bible. But I know if I destroy this land, if I destroy the sacred sites, I've got to suffer the consequences afterwards. We'll fight politically, we'll fight violently. If necessary we will use force to retain that park. I know black's, and I know young blacks are prepared to do that. A lot of other blokes would probably go along with them. But after that point of time, if we are defeated, we won't be defeated for ever.'

. . . .

'Already people have announced to me that they are prepared to get in front of the bulldozers if any of the trees were touched. They will not stand aside and let it happen. It is quite obvious from what's been told me that the people are intending to fight. Anything that we have gained within Brisbane, throughout Australia, has only come through the blacks' struggle. So they have got nothing to lose, and a lot to gain.'

. . . .

'Musgrave Park is the heart of the community. We like to sit amongst the trees with our people. We couldn't go to a hall, we don't feel relaxed and we can't come out and say what we really want to say. But if we sit in Musgrave Park they will speak out, and then speak out in all honesty. To me Musgrave Park is the heart of Brisbane'.

. . . .

'Musgrave Park is identified by my people as a place where they could feel secure in their role as the Aborigines – even though it's a negative at this stage. But they are secure with each other because of their identification with an Aboriginal area, and I suppose this is a major attraction, the sense of belonging because of the Aboriginal area that is identified with Musgrave Park.'

. . . .

I've been in Brisbane for the last 26 or 27 years before any of these black organisations were formed, we used it as a gathering place for black people. Now if you go to Musgrave Park today you'll see black people sitting there. It's an information centre for blacks from all over Australia – or anywhere, in Queensland – who come to Brisbane looking for their friends; they go to Musgrave Park because that's the information centre. But there's something in Musgrave Park. I can understand it. *You* can't, and you can't help it because you're white. But there's something very spiritual within us in Musgrave Park. There's not a month goes by when I don't jump in my motorcar and it's two miles to Musgrave Park, and sit there at two o'clock in the morning, and sit in a *bora* ring and speak and get the feeling from my ancestors and people who who still live within me today. And to get strength and to get that closeness, I do go to Musgrave Park for that and that alone. And how I keep carrying on is because I get that strength from within myself from those people.'

. . . .

'Musgrave Park serves as a haven or a refuge for nearly all black people. So where we can't reach into white society and draw strength from white society when we're down, we can reach back into black society and draw strength from there. And the only place we can go where we can touch our mother the earth, and feel the grass and the earth and see the trees and the birds in the sky, is Musgrave Park. It's the only place where we can gather socially and be accepted. You go into a white hotel or a white restaurant, or something like this, and many's the time you get rejected, or refused entry, for all sorts of reasons. They're very particular in the way they refuse you, and say, "Oh, you're wearing brown shoes, we are only allowed allowing people who wear black shoes today – it's not because you're black, don't get me wrong. You're not wearing a tie, we are only allowing people in here wearing a tie". Things like this.'

. . . .

'A lot of our old drones, that means old alcoholics, old "goomies", old metho kings and queens who passed on – like my sister who was classed as the Queen of the Drones of Queensland – died in Musgrave Park. We had a service for her in Musgrave Park. Only three weeks later we had another service for an old bloke from Cherbourg at Musgrave Park, and that is very good. We just don't say, "Have a service at Musgrave Park".

This old gentleman died about 200 miles away from here but he used to be in Musgrave Park, and the idea came from his own sons and daughters. We would like a service to be held for our father in Musgrave Park. So it is something spiritual drawing them back to Musgrave Park to have the service there. There are a lot of services held there, a lot of demonstrations; there have been a lot of communications there. You know, when the blacks want to get together, today, tomorrow or next week, they call a meeting in Brisbane and right throughout south-east Queensland here, and so, there's got to be a meeting in Musgrave Park. Blacks come from all around, and demonstrate and sit there to hear what the plan is. It's a place for people together, and Pastor Don Brady – to me he was the black Martin Luther King of Australia – he started his ministry there. He started to preach from Musgrave Park, and we used to have the police and what people driving past and they said, "What's this black fella doing speaking about the gospel of the Lord Jesus Christ – and he's speaking about land rights, and he's speaking about tribal areas. What's this man doing, this crazy man"? But let me tell you, the black people have sweet bugger all here in Brisbane, and all the service we get here in Queensland started from Musgrave Park! Musgrave Park is the gathering place for people.

. . . .

'When a black child is three or four years old, he's cute, he's a good mate for little white kids to play with, he can't do anything wrong. But as soon as he starts to get bigger and stand out a bit, the white parents generally say to the child, "Don't bring that little black kid home any more". The little white kid – it's his best mate – he gets all upset and says, "Why not"? But there's no explanation from mum and dad. There is an explanation that's detrimental to the black person – "The blacks are dirty, they've got nits in their hair, they all sleep together, and all sorts of things, and it's very down putting to the Aboriginal people, and there's no respect for our culture, our way of life". As the black kid grows up he can't hit out as anyone else, only himself for being black. And he sees this continual rejection, continual animosity that is directly attributable to his blackness.

And so he hates being black. The only release he has for this is through alcohol or drugs, and so the next step is alcohol and drugs. Then he overcomes this, but the feeling of not belonging, of being unacceptable, still stays with him, still lingers there. There's no incentive for him to improve his way of life, the only place you can turn to that is familiar to him where he feels at home, where he can forget all this, is Musgrave Park. And sure a lot of people drink there. But if you want to run the groups that are sitting there in the spark, you'll find that a lot of them aren't drinking but just sitting there talking, discussing the events that are occurring in relation to our people. It's just a social gathering on a lot of occasions. But the white man doesn't see this. He sees a group of blacks sitting there, so naturally assumed they were drinking and plotting all sorts of mischief. The white police believe this also, now you see them continually going there with their paddy-wagon's and just grabbing blacks left, right and centre whether they're drunk or not, putting them in jail and charging them with drunkenness – and so it goes on.'

. . . .

'When I came to Brisbane the first place I hit was Musgrave Park because I didn't know anyone around the place. I met a couple of people on the road, and the first thing they said was, "You'll see all the Murris down at Musgrave Park. So I just went down there and that all my people from where I came from.'

. . . .

''ve been living in the park for a year and a half to two years. Fifty or sixty people were living there. We had tents and everything. A couple of times the police cut the ropes so the tent fell down. Most of the time they come to hassle us. Sometimes when we are asleep they put their sirens on to wake us up or high beam their lights in our faces. You get some white people coming around to stir us up for sleeping in the park at 12 o'clock or 1 o'clock in the morning. They throw stones at us and bottles while we're asleep. It isn't much good, but it's the only place where we can live.'

. . . .

'My father used to live in Brisbane years ago, before he had any of his eleven children, and when he moved back in the early 1960s, South Brisbane was still thickly populated with Aboriginal and Islander people, particularly Aboriginal people, at my father would run into destitute lost souls, lost between two cultures, losing their own identity. And they're be drunk, hopelessly lost, didn't know what to do with their lives, living on the fringe so to speak. And he would know these people, and bring them home and would feed them and bath them and change their clothing. Before we knew it he was running more or less a hostel for people living in the South Brisbane area.'

. . . .

'Unfortunately white people can never understand the beauty, the closeness, of being black. When you are black, you are never alone. You see, a stranger can come into town, broke, with just the clothes he stands up in. He'll head for Musgrave Park and tell his story to some of the people there. Well, somebody will befriend him, take him home, give him a shower, change of clothes, a bed, and he's right till he gets on his feet.'

. . . .

'I think it's the spirit of the family of Brisbane of the Aboriginal community. If I was to go back there now, the only place that I would go back to first establish my place in that society is Musgrave Park. There I would be able to find my position within the community. It would be established there. If I wanted to meet anybody, that's where I'd have to go. If I was going to get any directions about what road I should travel or what I was going to do in relation to the struggle, or community development or to find out what the community wanted, it would be there. It's a grapevine that continually works for you. It's a place where you meet your family and stay. Your spirit is lifted again, your respect has come back.'

. . . .

'People truly don't understand the significance of the South Brisbane area. Suburban Aboriginals are still very much a cultural people and a spiritual people, and we've got our ties to that day and age and it's been passed down through generations. And the only bit of land, I'd unoccupied land, at the moment is Musgrave Park and we feel very strongly about this area. It's very spiritual as well, we've still got that tie, and would like to keep Musgrave Park as part of our ancestry, so to speak.'

. . . .

'Europeans and their perception of land is based on the materialistic. They look upon land as "My land, I own that land. It is a commodity". Whereas Aborigines look at something as part of the whole, a part of themselves, they are part of that – the land. The land and they are one. This is my perception of Musgrave Park – as an unspoiled segment of a once great spiritual piece of land that has been spiritual to a large number of tribes from this specific area of Australia. This is how I perceive Musgrave Park, and it is also a haven for me, where I can be an Aborigine without stress, without being ridiculed by Europeans, and being looked down on as sub-human by Europeans. It's a sense of being me, within my own environment. This is what Musgrave Park means to me.'

. . . .

Permission was expected [in 1990] for Aborigines to build a cultural centre on Musgrave Park which they would control. They hope that sometime in the future the whole park will be controlled by an Aboriginal Council. They say, 'This park to us is like Ayers Rock to the Central Australian Aborigines '.

UPDATE ON THE STATUS OF MUSGRAVE PARK

On 24 August 1998, after twenty years of legal struggles with the Queensland state government, the Musgrave Park Aboriginal Corporation (MPAC) secured a lease to build a cultural centre on portions of the park. The park holds special significance to the local indigenous population due to a past restriction barring Aborigines from crossing the park and entering the city of Brisbane notably, being the site of a buried *bora* ring it has historically been a sacred site to the native Murri people.

Each year, the park hosts the Paniyiri Greek Festival, the National Aboriginal and Islander Day of Celebration (NAIDOC) Park Day, and the Lesbian and Gay Brisbane Pride Festival Fair Day.

In 2020, the last day of National Reconciliation Week was marked by a candlelight vigil in Musgrave Park on 3 June 2020, with 432 candles lit for the each of the Aboriginal deaths in custody since the 1991 end of the Royal Commission into Aboriginal Deaths in Custody, and an extra one for George Floyd, an Afro-American man killed by a police officer in the United States.

10

Women of the Land

In 1995 ABC Books published this book based on transcripts of Ros' taped interviews with remarkable women working on the land all over Australia.

To give some idea of the richness of this project I have selected the story of one of the twenty-four women that featured in Ros' project. Alas, the book is no longer available. But this story illustrates the spirit and courage of all the rural women featured in Ros' documentaries and indeed this book.

The idea for this book came from ABC Radio's Rural Department, which in 1994 launched the ABC Rural Woman of the Year Award, and I was delighted when Nina Riemer of ABC Books approached me to interview a number of farming women who had participated in the inaugural award. For many years I had been involved with oral history for broadcast – both for ABC Radio National's Social History Unit, and before that The Coming Out Show – and Nina's idea was for me to interview a number of the women who is remarkable stories of courage and achievement had been uncovered by the Award.

I travelled all over Australia to interview the women on tape and Nina edited the transcribed types in such a way as to retain the character and the voice of the speakers – a technique she has used successfully another ABC book based on Social History Unit programs.

By happy coincidence, Mark Cranfield, head of the Oral History Section at the National Library of Australia, had indicated to me his interest in non-metropolitan subjects, so the master tapes and transcripts of interviews will be added to the Library's collection. Their generous support contributed significantly to the project's success. Some of the women I interviewed were already leaders in their rural communities and active in farmers' organisations, others were battlers on small subsistence farms but they all had stories to tell. I hope this book can bring more of their experiences to the attention of the general public and perhaps help bridge the gap of understanding between city and country. I hope it will also give recognition to the essential role played by women in Australia this rural industries.

Thanks are due to the staff of the ABCs Rural Department for their advice and for making telephone and other facilities available to me, to Dawn Webb, Isabelle Fogarty and Rose Eagleton who transcribe the tapes so speedily, also to the people of the ABC Ultimo switchboard who cheerfully connected me to a string of country numbers often early in the morning or at night.

But, most of all, I thank the rural women for their patience as my microphone intruded into their busy days and for making me welcome. And also for the many images of rural life which I could not record but which will stay in my memory.

Ros Bowden Sydney, June 1995

MURIEL DICK

Ros: Muriel Dick says she's greedy for living, and that old age is a myth! At 73 she runs the farm in southern Victoria by herself and takes an energetic interest in everything that comes her way, from new farming techniques to politics and world news. Her cattle are very fortunate, she respects they're natural instincts and allows them to roam between paddocks leading a sort of alternative lifestyle.

My mother came from Omeo; they were farmers but she married a man of the city. He was a carpenter in the Railways actually and when he retired he went up to Warburton and bought 20 acres, split them up into little housing blocks, build houses on them and soldl them off. I was his laborer, which I didn't mind at all because it gave me a terrific lot of freedom and he was very proud of me, which gave me a sort of self assurance: he gave me strengths that usually are given in the a male world. I had two dancing classes – skipping around and riding racehorses. It was a wonderful teenage life.

So you had no gender stereotype; you weren't forced to conform to one thing or another as a child.

Not really, and I think that's where I get my strengths from now. Back in my day women suffered a bit from being pinpointed but it didn't seem to worry me: I just sailed through life.

Did you learn carpentry from him, too?

No, I don't think so. I could drive a nail and I could saw but outside of that I don't think so. I think I was just filling in time and doing what he wanted me to do, because he adored me. He had lost his older son when he was 11 in an accidental drowning, and of course, the focus came on me then. There were others behind but they were quite a bit younger so I had a few privileges.

Was it marriage that brought you to the country?

Yes, although when I first got married we lived in East Melbourne my husband had come from farming stock and he really wanted to get back into the country. We didn't have any money, so we had to start from scratch, but when he sold his slow racehorses he had a little bit of capital and he leased a property. Then one day we were talking and he said, 'I would like a property'. All the farmers owned their farms or were on the way to owning them and we had a certain pride and I said, 'Yes, okay, that's what I want too', so we went for it. We just channelled everything into moving into properties. Yesterday I was on a 40 acre property that we owned once and I didn't know, because a new house has been built on it. The Women on Farms had a gathering there yesterday and it was a nice feeling, stamping around that ground.

When did you own this first property of yours?

About thirty years ago, perhaps more. We bought two little properties, one twenty acres and one thirty, sold those and bought here, which is eighty. My husband's brother lived on 100 acres down the road and he died but because it had to go through bloodlines his wife couldn't inherit. My husband got half and his sister got half. Then he bought her half but there was a debt on the property and he payed that debt to the widow, and that was like buying his share.

Was your husband a veteran of World War II?

No, he didn't go to the war. He lost two brothers in the First World War and I think there was that bit of heartache in the family and they were against war then. I don't know how he managed to get out of all these things but he thought he was too old in the Second World War, because he's quite a bit older than me: he's about nineteen-and-a-half years older than me. Everybody was so surprised when they found out how old he was because they thought he was only a few years older – but he joined me, I didn't join him. It was a good marriage to this extent: that we both were able to grow in our own way without being intruded upon.

So when you moved on to a farm, you'd had no real experience of farming?

Para not really. It was just as well we didn't go dairying when I had these those two young children they were twenty months apart. My son was born about eleven-and-a-half months after we were married and then twenty months after that a daughter – I was overwhelmed. I can remember wanting to get home from hospital so much… so quickly, to share this little boy baby with my husband, though when I did and I said, pick him up, he said, 'Oh, no, that's your responsibility'. I cried with disappointment. He walked around, looking me over, and said, 'Look even a heifer can look after it's calf!' I was devastated (laughs). I had the weight of responsibility on my shoulders, but then I gave over to the children so that's what I did for those years.

When we bought the twenty acres and the forty acres, my father, the carpenter came over and put up a funny little shed to milk cows in, and that's when we started dairying. We got a little herd together and I help then, and that's when it all started. I got quite fond of the cows. I could pat them and talk to them, and I found I had an affinity with them, and I was glad. It filled in some part of my life, actually. My children were off to school, that was the parting.

So you took charge of the dairy. Were there any other crops or other cattle on the property?

My husband used to get jobs here in there but no, not really. I think we must've looked pretty poor but I used to knit, sew, cook, garden; I was very energetic, so I didn't even notice that because my life is so full. I've been like that all my life I seem to be sort of able to make the best of that is and I pour all my energies into making it better.

Did you take charge while he was at work?

No, I wouldn't say that. He was the dominant factor; he was the one who knew it all. I was always two paces behind, giving all the support. He used me like a cattle dog –'Go way back, stop that bull, stand your ground, woman' – oh my god, with this great thing thundering at you! (Laughs). But I soon learned to cope with all that. I just picked it up myself. I was quite ignorant after he died. I used to stand around while he was up the windmill doing things; I wasn't very interested in that because being a kept woman I was out playing golf and just helped. My place was in the house really, and the garden, and with the children, but when he needed help, you know, you worked like a dog .(Laughs).

My life really centred around my children, my house, my garden, out there in the community, following the children through school. They went on to Scouts, Guidess, pony clubs, cricket, football, all that sort of thing, and I used to run them about. I was very keen, very ambitious, for my children to move on and I gave them all the support. So it was up to me; he was quite happy about that situation but when he needed help I have to be out there. Para I played golf for about 25 years, I suppose, and I was captain, president, handicap manager, running the show. It was great. How do I used to be the one that put on the school concerts and things like that. I trained quite a lot of debutant sets, and that took me right into the Young world, which was good, because I loved dancing. Of course it was country dancing back in those days.

What happened to the farm when your husband died?

Well, it was left to me eventually, after a bit of controversy about, 'You don't leave farms to women; they lose it, they will get married again and the guy will take off with it again' – all this sort of talk. This was his attitude, and I said, 'Okay, what about if I should die before you? You'd have somebody in to do the housework because you know what you're like with house work, and before you knew where you were you were you'd have her into bed, and where's my half then'? I think he had to think about that one, and then he said, 'Oh yes, I think you're right'. I don't think he was very sure of how I could manage, but I did – I'm still here!

I remember the day of his funeral – he died fourteen years ago – I went to the back door and stood in the sun for a minute and felt bereft; I felt as though I was in the world on my own. I thought, I don't know how I'm going to keep going, how can I walk. The little back gate was open and I thought I'd better shut that, so I walked down towards it. Then the thought came floating through, well at least I'm standing up and I'm walking. I determined then that I would create a pathway for myself and walk along that alone, and I did.

You were a helper on the farm but did you know anything about running it? How did you begin to run it?

One thing that stood in my favour was that he was rotten with figures and books so I had the books to do, although I could never write a cheque for myself without standing on the mat and demeaning myself by asking for money – I think all women were in that situation in my day, and still are. So I had a good, functional idea of how things run. I was pretty shrewd in a lot of ways, too, because I was aware of what we were trying to do with paying off the properties and getting there. I knew how to channel money and move in that direction so I had a lot of years of experience in my favour.

A friend of my husband from the Department of agriculture came and said, 'We'll go through your herd and we'll put ear tags in there is for identification'. He showed me how to keep information on them all in a folder, and from then on I could identify the cows and when they calved I could write down the carving date and whether the calf was male or female. I had a column for anything they were treated for or anything that went wrong.

That wasn't without a lot of pain and a lot of thinking and a lot of growth. I grew very rapidly through these years. I wouldn't like to go back there again, but there's no way in the world I would've missed this journey. It's been wonderful, because what I've really done is walk into myself; I found myself as a person. It was a very painful journey but it can be done. You don't die; you suffer a lot of pain, but you get there if you want to.

Did you find people were encouraging you to keep the farm, or did they say you should sell it and go into the town?

I remember playing golf with a woman who was into Yoga, and she said with a smile in her eyes and her voice, 'Muriel, you know 99.6 per cent of women in your position would sell and go to live in the town'. She was quite amused about the fact that I was the sole operator on the farm out there. I said, 'No I'd shoot myself within a week. (Laughs.)

I like the challenges so that's how it was. But if it hits your pocket you learn very quickly. I don't know that I had too many disasters – I was too careful for that with my background of years of getting it together. I just thought about it and when I made my moves I seemed to be doing the right thing all the time, and I did it my way, too. I think a lot of farmers are quite brutal with cattle. I'm not judging them; it's just a way of doing things from way back. But I'm tuned into nature and I'm very aware that we are only another species on this planet and you must have respect for everything on this planet, so I'm very caring with my animals.

What sort of practical things did you have to learn in relation to the cows?

Well my job is sort of checking out. I have pulled calves, although I'm not really mad about pulling calves and now that I've got to this stage I feel I don't need to do that. I know a lot of the vets and a lot of the Aricultural Department people think I'm mad, but I don't have to get the vet very often because of my method and my 'open gate philosophy'. I think a cow can look after it's calf better than I can. If she can move from one paddock if the winds blowing, or the rain or the sleet is coming from some other direction, she'll take her calf off and go beyond those trees over there. I've got wind breaks in most of the paddocks and this is what she does.

I'm into preventative health by putting what is been depleted out of their system into dishes around the paddocks – dishes in tyres so they don't knock them over. They calve stress free.

I will not have dogs chase my cattle. Some of the agents want to round them up but I say, 'No, I'll get them into the yards for you, or into the lane', so they made allowances. They come half an hour later and I have them in the lane and we just walk them up nice and quietly. They're all quiet; I can get out of my ute and walk all around them, bull and all, and tell him how nice he is, and he responds.

You're into an alternative lifestyle for your cattle.

Yes, I would say that. But let's be fair to other farmers; if they're young they have to move in an intensive farming method with each and every blade of grass to get the money to meet their commitments. I'm freehold and that takes a lot of pressure off me: all I do is keep upgrading my farm.

Do you go to farm open days and things like that and courses that the Agricultural Department runs?

I did the Beef Management course for twelve months, which was marvellous. There were seventeen guys to start with – a few of them dropped out – and three females and we all got so fond of one another that we met for months after at a restaurant just to say, 'Where are you at now'? It was great, but I wasn't interested in a lot of it. I still went back to my way of keeping books; I was a bit lost. It was an accredited course and I could've got a job if anybody wanted to employ me. I passed with flying colours and all that sort of thing but, no, I do it my way. I live my life my way, I can't help myself. It's something to do with being close to nature and reflecting everything on this earth and it seems to pay off with animal health, my health and so many things.

You're in your early seventies now. Is there anything that you can't do, or you don't do?

There are lots of things I can't do; actually, I'm very ignorant of a lot of things and I have to get a bit of help now. I can't service my ute but I can service my tractor. I've got an old Nuffield and I can change the oil and put in new filters and things like that because I did a course. Those courses are marvellous: they build up confidence.

I had two guys come here one time in the 1980s trying to flog me one of the latest tractors with all the computer systems and goodness knows what. I thought about it for a while but I haven't got the work for it even though I cut my own hay. I have all my own haymaking machinery. I go on the mower, I cut it, and then I have somebody come in to rake ahead of me and then I bale. But then I use contractors to cut it. I'm into square bales still because it suits me. I've been cutting my own paid for fourteen years or more now, and yet, it's a funny thing, I always go on the rake for my husband and I used to say to him occasionally, 'Let me go on the baler', but he'd say, 'Oh, no, no, this is too complicated!' The fellows around here laugh because I twiddle with knobs – God only knows what they're about but I twiddle with them – and I get the results because I just tune into what I'm doing. I'm very careful of my machinery because I pay for it if it breaks down.

So you've got your own methods of irrigating?

It's not really irrigating, is it? It's just filling the trough. I just use the old pipes from the irrigation system out of the big diesel engine to pump up water into the tank to keep the supply up.

You're very involved with women's groups and things around here. What brought you into that?

Even before I did a few skilling courses at the McMillan Rural College they said they were trying to put skilling courses for women into place and would I help them? They wanted to know what my needs were, so I said, well, I suppose pulling a calf, say; fixing a fence; fertilisers; how to recognise weeds from good grasses. They were working these things on this whiteboard and then they said something about driving a tractor, and I said, 'Oh, I know how to drive a tractor so I don't want that one'. 'But other women might', and I said, 'Yes'. Then they said, do you want a job? I thought I had enough to do, but even back then I was into empowering women – I think I've been in it all my life. That's the thread that keeps me going a lot in another dimension, to empower women to take control of their own lives, to be responsible for themselves and to grow up. So I did, and it was great.

Tell me about the women's group you go to.

It's a continuation of women on farms. All we do is meet, we go round to a farm a month and anyone can put up ideas. We are non-hierarchical, we are co-operative and if any woman has anything to offer we don't care whether she's got one acre or a thousand acres, and we let them all know that, because some of them are a bit tentative, with not much confidence. They're growing very quickly and they're not frightened to put their ideas forth and we listen. Some of them we bag, 'That's a rotten idea'! or whatever, but we're going from strength to strength, which is good.

We go onto the property – we've been on alpacas, emus, ostriches, dairy farms, rotolacs with five or six hundred cows. We've been down to a Simmental stud we talk to vets and they tell us about all sorts of things to educate us and give us insights into what's going on. I'm not impressed with a lot of the stuff. They push the barriers to far with two big-framed animals and they cause the female to break down in the birthing area.

Is it a discussion group where you discuss things like education and the concerns of countrywomen?

Not really, because there's a big range of women out there. Some haven't moved along and some have moved along very quickly, so we've got to be careful because some are stuck in all the different places where I was once stuck in life.

Do you see changes?

Yes, mighty changes! Some of the women at first were under the influence of their husbands but now they've moved out of the shadows into the sunshine a bit. You can see in their faces that they've moved along somewhat, the penny has started to drop and they're taking a bit more control of their own lives. But we're not political, really. Why do I say that? Well they're also busy with their own affairs on a personal level.

I get phone calls from all over the place saying, 'Come to a meeting', but I cannot go to meetings and run this project so I have to get my priorities in order. What do I want to do? Well I don't really want to get out there because that's not really me, sitting around at meetings I'm just talking, this is really me, on the farm, doing all these horrible jobs.

You look very fit. What do you see your future being on the farm?

To be quite honest, I live in the present. At seventy-three years of age I wouldn't say I do have a great long future so I live in the moment, and my movements are so full that it's wonderful. I'm really living about six lives in the moment. I seem to get around a lot of things. I try to read about the things I'm interested in – there's a lot of literature that comes through that I should be reading, but I don't.

I'm moving ahead, somewhere ahead, I don't know where because I'm interested in women developing and growing and taking their place in life with full responsibility for themselves in a lot of areas. That's not at the expense of fellows – I'm always saying this – because I've got a son and I love him and I had a husband and they were all stuck, like a lot of women are stuck.

But you're moving through?

I'm moving through. I've walked out of the shadows into the sunshine. Actually, that day I was telling you about when I walked that path, I walked along the path out of the shadows into the sunshine and into myself as a person. That was the most rewarding thing I've ever, ever done.

You're also challenging age a bit.

Yes, but I'm not actually challenging it because I recognise that you've got to die and you're not going to function one hundred per cent like when you were young. I accept all that but I'm going to fully live until I do die because I love life. I've lost all my religious leanings and I've tapped into life. The closest I can get to the meaning of life is the life force and that's a mystery. There's a life force of all the species and it all comes from the one source. That's a wonderful feeling, that's life force that invigorates and live and you, and I recognise it and respect it.

You don't think as you lie in bed in the morning, well, I'm seventy-three years old now it's my turn to take things a bit easy?

Never, never, never! No, for the simple reason that I talk to so many women in the town and I can look into their lives. Women much younger than I am – say, fifty-one, fifty-two – and they are bored out of their brains. They're not really fully living. They've got to be racing around. They live their lives around shopping centres trying to fill up the day, or playing bingo – fancy that now sitting playing bingo. I would be bored stiff!

11

Penelope Heads West

Ros Bowden was one of the early interviewers and contributors to The Coming Out Show (it's earliest title was The Coming Out – Ready or Not – Show) which began in 1975, a weekly 45-minute radio magazine program which broke new ground, and although first broadcast because of the International Women's Year and was only intended to run for a week, it ran for twenty years.

Julie Rigg was one of its first co-ordinators.

'The show happened because the Whitlam Labor Government wanted a Women's Adviser and kept asking several statutory authorities what they were doing about International Women's Year. I recall an internal ABC memo at the time saying, "Why don't we give the girls a week". One of the producers, Liz Fell, got together with me and Gillian Waite, and we said, "We don't want to be token, we want a year".'

But as mentioned, *The Coming Out Show* ran for twenty years, and it tackled once fringe issues in the mainstream media, like abortion law reform, adoption, domestic violence, women's music, arts and theatre, women's history, health and nutrition, as well as political and social issues affecting women in Australia and overseas.

The program was also broadcast over the ABC's Third Network, to rural and outback areas, triggering one listener from Kempsey to write, 'Without *The Coming Out Show* it was difficult for women in country areas to stay aware of what was happening and what other women were thinking and doing'. She concluded, 'Women in rural areas are isolated and this program is a great relief from the drought'.

One of the early producers, Nicola Joseph, had a background in working for the Macquarie University-based, volunteer-staffed radio station 2SER. 'I was also the only one who was a person of colour. 'That was really distressing for me because I had applied for other jobs against people who were just as experienced as me. But Sydney was a very white

Geraldine Doogue and Eva Cox.

First home erection at Northbridge of the newly purchased *The Manor*.

place at that time. So for me, joining the Women's Unit was an opportunity to actually get a job in the ABC, something that was difficult to get, in my position.

Ros also worked for 2SER.

Nicola Joseph: 'I came from an Arabic background so Sydney was quite a difficult place to work culturally as an Arab, so the Women's Unit was really a very supportive environment and the programming was inspiring. I had been a feminist for years, and *The Coming Out Show* was an important program with a lot of value.'

Julie Rigg: 'A lot of our stuff was pretty rough. In the first place I had been a journalist in the 1960s, but not in radio. So we did stuff about rape and sexual violence, about adoption as a cruel social experiment and broadcasting a program from New Zealand where there was social experimenting in which children from poor families were transferred to the rich. We broadcast stories about abortion and the right to work. In the 1960s we didn't have a guarantee to work. In the post-war, women had been pushed away so the men could come back and take their jobs.'

As part of celebrating 20 years of *The Coming Out Show* a one-off 'hypothetical' was broadcast, and Julie Rigg was asked what to expect.

'I was very interested in listening to a recent Radio National *Background Briefing* program on surrogacy. We actually broadcast the first programs on surrogacy in 1981 on *The Coming Out Show*. And in that program we predicted the fact that poor coloured women in countries that weren't industrialised would have to carry the children of rich white women. There was a segment in the satirical film *The Life of Brian* when one of the guys said, "I want to have a baby". His friend replied, "You can't have a baby, where are you going to put it – in a box"? That was as far as they predicted, but we did see that this is still an unresolved issue. I do have this idealistic view that we need to know the conditions of women in other countries. And Radio National has a very special role in that.

'The women I spoke to about the *in vitreo* program in Melbourne were divided on the surrogate issue. So many people talk about re-organising genetics, putting embryos into other people and growing a different race of people. I just don't feel that in countries, especially like Australia, where we are educated thinking people who, on the whole, would provide the number of bodies needed. It was very clear to me which way this was going to go. And that's a good example of the collaboration between *The Coming Out Show* and the Science Unit about the time of the first test-tube baby.

'Now there are 12,000 or 13,000 babies born by IVF each year in Australia. So we've come a long way.'

. . . .

In 1994 when I retired from the ABC (after Ros fired me – well in a manner of speaking) after encouraging me to take redundancy. I still had a couple of major projects to do which included writing the history of the of the Australian Antarctic Division to mark its 50th anniversary *The Silence Calling – Australians in Antarctic, 1947-97*, plus a six-part television travel-adventure series on the same theme, *Breaking the Ice* for ABC-TV. Ros continued her freelancing with the ABC for the Social History Unit and in by 1998 had started a two-year course for a Diploma of Horticulture at Sydney TAFE. (I reminded her of the old Dorothy Parker line, *You can lead a whore-to-culture, but you can't make her think*, to which she responded with a rather tired smile as it was not the first time I had used this quote.) This had happened at a moderately inconvenient time, as we had recently bought a second-hand Toyota diesel Landcruiser, and a Jayco 'Flight' camper in which we hoped to do some long-distance touring in the Wide Brown Land.

That meant our first excursion across the Nullarbor Plain to the south of Western Australia had to be sandwiched into the two-month December and January university and indeed TAFE annual vacation, now that our two sons, Barnaby and Guy, who were now in their early twenties could be left to their own devices.

The purchase of our Landcruiser was a big step from our split-screen Kombi and 4 X 4 trailer in which we had taken both our sons to the outback when they were eight and eleven. The Jayco 'Flight' was the smallest in the pop-up off-road camper range, which collapses down into a compact trailer for easy towing. At the end of the day you wound it up with a crank handle, pulled beds out at each end, and the whole thing expanded miraculously like Dr Who's Tardis. Inside was a stove, fridge, two bench seats and a table. We fell in love with it at a caravan and camping show in Sydney where we intended just to look. Ten minutes later (it seemed) we were signing up for a new one. Roz thought it was such a luxurious way to camp that she instantly christened it *The Manor.* 'OK', sez I, I said, sensing as one often does in a relationship that the decision was final. 'But what about the Landcruiser'?

Our genial salesman put his oar in.

'You'll have to call the Landcruiser *Penelope.*' He was referring to a long-running television comedy series the ABC was running in those days, called *To The Manor Born,* which starred the formidable Penelope Keith and her co-star Peter Bowles. I twigged the connection quickly enough.

'But Ros, we simply can't have a four-wheel-drive called Penelope!

'Why not'?

'What about my macho outback image? People might laugh and point...'

Ros was merciless. 'You haven't got one anyway.'

Penelope and *The Manor* it was and remained so.

. . . .

'Look – it's a dunny in a tree!

Well, it was on a fence-post actually. Heading west in early December towards the Western Australian border on the Eyre Highway you begin to run out of barbed-wire as the last of the parched, marginal sheep country gives way to unfenced Mallee scrub, and then to open saltbush plainss with no trees at all – the true Nullarbor Plain.

Ros had spotted it. I was driving Penelope, lost in my thoughts and semi-hypnotised by the dead straight ribbon of bitumen ahead.

'Are you sure'?

'Yes'!

'Can't be'.

Ros was cocky. 'Bet you five bucks'.

Unusual roadside sculpture on the Nullarbor Plain.

Hijacked Santa in the Fowlers Bay Mail truck.

We were about two kilometres on by then, with Penelope towing The Manor at a steady cruising speed of 100 km/h. The road was clear fore and aft, and I slowed down, did a U-turn and headed back. They had to be a photograph in it at least.

And there it was – a ceramic toilet bowl perched perkily on a fence-post, nicely offset by a photogenic dead Mallee branch. Perhaps it had fallen off the proverbial truck? Or had some mad surrealist artist taken it out there as a free-form outback sculpture? One of life's little unexplained mysteries, really. A travel vignette on which to ponder.

We were heading west in early December, but it was unseasonably cool. A week before it had been 45°C at Ceduna. Not the most sensible time of the year for outback travel, but we had no alternative. We have two months to explore the southern coast-line and south west corner of Western Australia – which we hope will not be a furnace –and return to Sydney. First we will follow the route that the explorer Edward John Eyre took in 1840, around the great Australian Bight from South Australia to King George Sound in Western Australia. We think of Edward John as we sit in air-conditioned comfort looking at the waterless, relentless, Mallee dotted landscape that nearly killed him and his party. Behind us rolls The Manor, 60 litres of water in her tank, all mod cons, plenty of tucker and comfortable beds waiting for us at the end of each day.

We weren't planning to camp in The Manor until after Port Augusta. The idea was not to linger in New South Wales on this part of the trip, because of time constraints, but to begin our journey to the west as close as possible to Ayer's 1840 exploratory push from the peninsula named after him, around the head of the Bight, to King George Sound (where Albany now is), keeping as close to the coast as practicable.

Because of our delayed exit from Canberra, we were happy to make it to Narrandera by dust, checking into one of the many excellent, economical motels in the town. It was hot, with the mercury still around 30°C. Electing for Chinese takeaway I went looking for a cold bottle of beer, and found myself having a surreal experience. The pub, in the centre of town, was admittedly small. It had cold beer on tap but none in bottles.

Nor did it sell any wine at all, hot or cold. 'Oh it's a terrible place, the pub with hot beer'.

Narrandera is on the Murrumbidgee, and on our way out the next morning we doubled back briefly to have a look out over the Narrandera Lake in the early morning light. At the turn of the century the Murrumbidgee Irrigation Authority was a major employer, constructing canals to carry precious water to the newly irrigated farms. The lake did not exist until 1925, and then only by accident. During the severe floods of May in that year, two small boys drilled a tiny hole into the main canal bank to see what sort of flow they could get. As it happened they got a good one. By the next day that section of the canal bank had collapsed. And the whole of the Bundidgerry flat was flooded. Bill Talbot, the Town Clerk of the day, suggested to the council that the flooded area be developed as a bathing and recreation area. It was named Lake Talbot in 1950 – without a plaque to the anonymous urchins who were really responsible.

It was going to be another hot one as we headed west across the Hay Plains – a cloudless, beautiful morning but with an ominous haze of bushfire smoke on the horizon. The lush green plains of the paddocks that were irrigated was a startling contrast to the white parched grass of those that were not. After Hay the country becomes even flatter and more featureless, with almost bare earth and stunted scrub seemingly stretching to infinity. The bitumen ribbon ahead was a shimmering mirage out of which huge trucks appeared, their tops seemingly detached by optical illusion, dominating the landscape in the absence of any trees. We passed the entrance to a property on our right appropriately named 'Hells Gates'.

There was some shade under peppertrees near a rather desolate artificial irrigation lake close to Euston. We stationed ourselves comfortably with our folding table and chairs and watched the pelicans paddle solemnly by as we hoed into fresh bread sandwiches bulging with corn beef and pickle. Stupidly I left a portable cold pack on the trailer bar, but it sat there rather miraculously without falling off. I noticed it when we swapped over the driving just passed the South Australian border. We are developing a routine of driving for two hours each to minimise driver fatigue. One of the advantages of a camping rig like The Manor, which tows as a low trailer rather than a caravan, is that you can cover long distances quickly when you want to.

The quarantine inspection on the border of South Australia and New South Wales was rigourous. But we were able to stock up with wonderful fresh fruit in Renmark on the roadside stall staffed by a cheerful Italian woman with only rudimentary English. Her family probably has probably been living in this area for generations. She insisted we sample the peaches, nectarines, apricots and even fresh figs.

Our next stop is Barmera, by Lake Bonney. And we will erect The Manor and not stay in a motel. What is the point of having plans if you don't change them? There are two Lake Bonneys in South Australia, both named after Ros' great-great-grandfather, the explorer Charles Bonnie and she is keen to investigate her ancestral connections.

I have a different interest in Barmera but it also has a Bonney link. Many years ago a friend in Adelaide sent me a priceless cutting from The Advertiser newspaper about a cultural event that took place in the Bonney Theatre in August 1978. Sure enough, there it was as we drove towards the lake-side camping ground. The story, in my view, is a minor classic that needs to be shared.

THE TIME TRUE ART CAME TO BARMERA

A tucker truck missed its cue at a theatre banquet in Barmera on Friday – and brought down the house.

The 280 guests at the Bonney Theatre, out for an evening of wining and dining and musical style entertainment, sipped on their pre-dinner drinks, unaware of the fate of the truck bringing the banquet.

Four hours later they were still sipping away – with disastrous consequences.

First of all the truck bringing the food from Adelaide had a series of flat tyres. Then the trailer was damaged, spoiling the food.

Back in the Bonney Theatre the evening organised by the Apex Club went on regardless.

A play, 'A Bards Banquet', *with players from the Arts Council of South Australia, was delayed to keep the acts in time with the scheduled banquet – but by 9 pm, when there was still no sign of the food, the curtain went up.*

According to the Arts Council touring manager Mr J Maxwell, the famished but lubricated crowd was rowdy, somewhat unruly, and beyond caring for the finer points of theatre.

An organiser mounted the centre stage to appeal for order, but was hit on the neck by a tomato. One of the audience quipped that the tomato should've been shared by the hungry audience.

Soup, hurriedly rustled up on the spot, was served soon after but when empty, the soup plates were hurled about the hall.

Mr Maxwell described the evening as 'a nightmare happening before my eyes'. He said the climax came when his cast left the stage and reported seeing an over-amorous couple staging their own performance in the gallery overlooking the audience.

A second couple was later seen 'having intercourse between courses'.

'It gave everyone something other than hunger to talk about', Barmera resident and one of the guests Mrs C Rooney, said last night.

The caterer finally arrived at 11 pm. Some of the food was promptly eaten, while the rest was disposed of as projectiles aimed at the actors on the stage.

The caterers did not charge. The guests paid $9 each. Drinks were extra. The St John Ambulance Brigade got about $2000 from the epic fundraiser.

I'm just grateful that my actors got through the night relatively unscathed, the Arts Council Manager Mr Maxwell said.

. . . .

We are camped on grass beside Lake Bonney, under gum trees clustered with larrikin white cockatoos which, for seemingly no reason, suddenly all take off and wheel about above us screeching in their usual ear-splitting way. They make the smaller clusters of pink and grey galah's sound quite pianissimo. Pelicans paddle past the shore line with stately unhurried calm, and the magpies mellifluous warbling calls can hardly be heard against the competition. Flocks of other water birds can be seen in the distance across the lake to the west.

Ros reminds me that this is a re-run of the arrival of her great-great-grandfather Charles Bonney and his companion Joseph Hawdon when they came upon the lake in 1838. They were driving cattle from New South Wales to Adelaide – the first time this had been attempted. Hawdon noted in his diary, 'A fine lake of freshwater, about thirty miles in circumference', beside which they camped. Like us they arrived in the evening. They noticed some Aborigines camped further around the lake who were also aware of them. It was a beautiful moonlit night, and the two men strolled along the banks to shoot some of the thousands of ducks resting on the water. It had a spectacular effect, is the echoes of the shots 'rolled along the water magnificently – one would have supposed that a hundred shots had been fired at the same moment'. at that point all the water birds took off 'screaming and cackling with alarm at the novel sound'.

I'll bet all the Aborigines knew they were there after that!

Hawdon learned that the Aboriginal name for the lake was *Nookampka*, but on that same day named it Lake Bonney 'after my friend and fellow traveller Mr M C Bonney whose company contributed so much to the pleasure of my expedition'.

When Ros told her aunt Nora Bonney about our intended journey, she said we would be passing Lake Bonney, which triggered Ros' interest in finding out more about her explorer great-great-grandfather. Like Edward John Eyre (with whom he was friendly) Bonney was an engaging young Englishman who arrived in Australia with the idea of making something of himself – that was sustained by a strong sense of adventure. Bonney was twenty-one when he arrived in New South Wales in 1834, first to work as a judges' clerk in Sydney, but his restless spirit soon had him employed on a new pastoral property on the Murray River. His employer, C H Ebden, asked him to try to find a practicable stock route to the new Port Philip settlement, and after a couple of attempts he got through in 1837. At that time the Port Philip settlement (as it was called then) consisted of a few huts with one newly erected weatherboard store, conspicuous by its fresh coat of paint amongst the ruder habitations by which it was surrounded. To get back to Sydney, Bonney first had to sail across Bass Strait to Launceston – from which city, of course Melbourne had been settled. As a former Tasmanian, I think it's important to remind Melburnians of this.

When Bonney got back to Sydney he set off south again with another mob of cattle – keeping a wary eye out for bushrangers – pioneering the route he first called The Sydney Road and is today known as the Hume Highway.

With the summer twilight stretching ahead, a proudly erected The Manor and our beds ready for later use, we decided to explore and eat out at the historic Overland Corner Hotel beside the Murray River. Driving around the eastern shore of the lake we stopped by the ruined stone walls of another hotel, built in 1859 after Bonney and Hawdon had found a way through the complex waterways feeding the Murray. The information plaque reminded us that this was not exploration for exploration's sake, but hard-edged commercial pastoral opportunism. Charles Sturt and Edward John Eyre (contemporaries of Hawdon and Bonney) also made their reputations as early Australian explorers by droving cattle into unknown country.

We found the Overland Corner hotel some twelve kilometres further on. It's a delightful blend of National Trust property and a local hostelry. Its small stone rooms and inner courtyard are stuffed with fascinating historical bric-a-brac. On the window ledge beside us in the bar are a couple of early irons. One was fairly basic, designed to be filled with hot coals or charcoal – it even had a little chimney built on the sharp end. But the other, more technologically advanced iron was quite alarming, with a metal bulb on the rear end surrounded by a Primus mechanism and powered by petroleum. I kept imagining all the catastrophes to garments and the users, and the inadvertent housefires that it must have ignited. Medallions for bravery should have been issued by the manufacturers to the housewives of the day who attempted to use it.

The Overland Corner hotel was flooded almost to the roof as recently as 1956. The waterline high up on the wallpaper can be seen clearly. It's either a flood or a famine in outback Australia. Our excellent steaks were washed down with equally delicious local South Australian red and our talk turned to Charles Bonney. After his early success in taking cattle overland it to Port Philip, Bonney had become an expert bushman and drover and he jumped at the chance to join Joseph Hawdon in his plan to drive cattle from New South Wales to Adelaide in 1838.

'He was very good at avoiding conflict with Aborigines', said Ros. 'He used to play his flute to help overcome difficult situations'.

'Really'?

Ros said this apparently unlikely tactic is confirmed in an account of his 1838 journey written by Joseph Hawdon, who was also adept at avoiding conflict. On 6 March at the end of a hard days droving, Hawdon stripped off and went down to the river to have a drink. As he came out of the water he was somewhat alarmed to see five Aborigines standing on the bank about fifteen metres above him, leaning on their spears. Not sure of their intentions, Hawden decided to clown his way out of trouble, 'commenced a dance, as a little merriment will at any time drive all hostility from their minds'. Once he had picked up his guns, 'which I had incautiously left on the side of the bank' he felt more in control of the situation.

Getting back to camp after his impromptu, pre-emptive pirouette, he found Charles Bonney has been approached by a larger group of Aborigines and was handling things in his own inimitable style by playing 'a few sweet tunes on his flute by the riverside' for an audience of about forty fascinated warriors. Hawdon was very taken with this – clearly a believer in the doctrine of 'the noble savage' – noted in his diary: 'I have often noticed that the finest-looking men are the fondest of hearing the music…'

Ros recalled that the author Ernestine Hill described Charles Bonney as 'a Pied Piper of the woodland' because of his penchant for entertaining 'both blacks and whites with his flute' writing that 'many a time he won a battle before it began by raising a general laugh'.

'I think my great-great-grandfather sounds very nice bloke', said Ros. He would've been a wonderful travelling companion'.

'For the moment', I said, 'you'll have to make do with me'.

The first sight of white men and their horned beasts must've been an alarming and bizarre site for the local tribes. Four days before the all-dancing, all-musical encounter, Hawdon and Bonney faced at least one hundred warriors, formed up in front of their women and children, who threatened the party with their spears and gestured that they should go away. The explorers and the cattle moved on, only to encounter another big, similarly feisty group of Aborigines blocking their way. Again humour saved the day, as the blacks surrounded the party with uncertain intentions.

One of the Aborigines asked Hawdon with suitable pantomime, whether the heifers in the flock were the wives of the white men? There was much laughter.

But a little later things became tense again, and when a warrior raised his spear while Hawdon's back was turned, he was nearly shot by one of the stockman. On this occasion the cattle save the day. Nervous at being surrounded they suddenly rushed – two of the beasts charging the blacks right and left, who saved themselves from being gored by their extreme agility. Hawdon noted that the cattle were very sensitive to the presence of Aborigines. 'Long before they could catch sight of the blacks they evidently knew of their approach by their smell, and would carry their heads direct in the air, and snort aloud'.

After they passed Lake Bonney the explorers had good reason to be grateful to two local Aborigines who acted as guides and saved the party many days of painful unnecessary travel. Bonney and Hawdon had to decide whether to drive the heavy drays along the river flats, or up on the cliffs which were often two or three hundred metres high. The river flats were firmer, but sometimes the explorers would come to a dead end on a bend of the river, where the river eroded into high cliffs. Bonney was amazed at the intelligence their Aboriginal guides displayed. 'Before they had been half a day with us they knew as well as we did where a dray could go and where it could not go, although they had never seen white men before. They never once made a mistake as to where we could keep to the flats and when we must take the high land'.

Bonney and Hawdon reached Adelaide in early April. Like Melbourne at that time, what was to be 'the city of churches' was then just a collection of basic wooden huts. The settlers were surprised and delighted –

particularly at the arrival of the overlanded cattle. Up till that time they had been living almost exclusively on kangaroo flesh.

. . . .

Onward and onward west along the Eyre Highway to Poochera, where we planned to turn southward to Streaky Bay. This would be Ros' second visit to Poochera, which if you blink is unlikely to be noticed.

There are the obligatory wheat silos, hotels, toilet-sized railway station, caravan park and roadhouse – not even a general store, which had burned down by the time Ros went there in 1994. But it has a heritage ant *Nothomyrmecia macrops*. Ros made a half-hour radio documentary about it for the ABC, as part of a series on important national heritage projects, produced in association with the Australian Heritage Commission.

How could you have made a half hour program about an ant?

It's a very interesting ant', said my partner firmly. 'What does it look like'?

'I'm told it is a pale yellow colour and has very large black eyes'.

'Do I gather that you have directly seen it then'?

'No'.

'You made a documentary about this unique ant at Poochera. You came here specially. But you didn't set eyes on one'?

'It is a prehistoric ant', said Ros, 'that has somehow miraculously survived in Australia. It's sometimes called the Golden Ant or the Dinosaur Ant because it's closest relatives were alive when they were, 100 million years or so ago. But it only comes out of its underground nest in the dark when it's freezing cold, to climb trees to find its food. When I got to Poochera it was winter. I thought there wasn't much point in getting up at 3 am to look for it and which wasn't going to make any noises for my tape recorder. I was after all, making a radio program.'

Ros did interview some locals about the ant, and later interviewed the scientist who had rediscovered it, Dr Bob Taylor, now living in Canberra. *Nothomyrmecia macrops* had become a kind of Holy Grail for entomologists since it had first been identified. That was an unusual enough story in itself.

In December 1931 a party of amateur naturalists set out from Balladonia Station to Israelite Bay on the south-east coast of Western Australia. The general collection of insects they found was then handed over to a remarkable woman, Amy Crocker, wife of the owner of Balladonia Station (which Ros and I planned to visit on our way west). Amy was a keen amateur naturalist and self-taught artist. She had a natural gift for drawing insects but did not, apparently, sketch either of the two specimens of *Nothomyrmecia* that had been fortunately collected. The insects gleaned on that 1931 – 32 expedition were sent to John Clark (a taxonomist at the Museum of Victoria) to formally describe the species and gave it the full name of *Nothomyrmecia* bastard, or (false bulldog ant) *macrops* (big eyes). The discovery caused worldwide scientific excitement because the golden ant represented an early stage of evolution, when ants were evolving from wasp ancestors.

But embarrassingly the golden ant slipped off the etymological map. No one could find it again in Western Australia or anywhere else. In 1977 an American entomologist said he was coming to Australia to try to locate *Nothomyrmecia macrops*. That dented national pride, so members of the CSIRO Division of Entomology Insect Taxonomy Group in Canberra, including Bob Taylor, decided to mount their own expedition. They headed for Western Australia, and on their way camped near Poochera about 10 pm, well short of the daily travel target. Although they were tired and frazzled from two long days driving, they immediately begin looking for insects, using helmets with battery lamps mounted on them.

It was October, it was cold, and a freezing wind was blowing in from the Southern Ocean. No one was finding anything terribly interesting and Bob Taylor decided the exercise was a dead loss. Their warm caravan beckoned, with the promise of a hot drink and a good book. On his way back his headlamp shone on a couple of tree trunks which were only about ten metres from the caravan.

As Taylor later told Ros, 'I thought, I'll just have a look there. I walked across. Immediately my lamp hit the tree lit up *Nothomyrmecia*. This was

1300 kilometres east of where we expected to find it, and obviously an enormous surprise.

Taylor rushed back to the caravan, calling out the good news. (Not 'Eureka! 'according to a colleague but, 'The bloody bastard's here)! Another entomologist Murray Upton, was working on a light sheet looking at some of the other insects located that night.

'He refused to believe the news until I tipped the ant out on the light sheet, and I'll never forget his eyes as he acknowledged that it was indeed *Nothomyrmecia*. It was a dramatic first encounter with a living fossil by anyone who could identify it. Taylor said until he woke up the next morning and saw the specimens again he couldn't be sure it wasn't a dream.

It seems that *Nothomyrmecia* is a very un-antish ant. These ants don't work as a team when foraging as most ants do, nor did they divide up the major jobs, with some individual specialising in foraging and others dedicated entirely to working inside the nest, looking after the larvae or storing food. The golden ant is an individualist, each worker sometimes labouring inside the nest, or at other times going out to forage. (The reason it only goes out on cold nights is to climb trees to sting and kill insects made torpid by the cold).

This singular ant is not capable of leaving scent-blazed trails to guide ants to a food source, its workers don't lick or groom their nest mates, and it has an ingenious ability to navigate its way to its food source and back to the nest by sight using the pattern of mallee branches silhouetted against the night sky like an ancient mariner's map.

Until Bob Tyler happened upon *Nothomyrmecia*, no local had ever seen it. 'If they had', said Taylor, 'they would probably have trodden on it'. The nests with found in a patch of mallee scrub, on a limestone outcrop, that had probably not been cleared for that reason.

There were further surprises. Another big group of golden ants was found in a Poochera yard containing a couple of sheds which had been used by truckies overnight on their long hauls across the continent. Nearby were all kinds of discarded junk, old cable drums, rusty tins and at one stage, Taylor discovered, a small pen with pigs in it. *Nothomyrmecia* was actually foraging on the trees, the bases of which were in the little pig pen. The area also had tracks all through it made by young people with their trail bikes.

Other patches of similar bush nearby yielded no *Nothomyrmecia.* We did find them in the Poochera rubbish dump. There we were, picking ants off the trees with our headlamps glinting on broken glass and the eyes of feral cats living in the rubbish tip. So *Nothomyrmecia* tolerates pretty disturbed conditions. There are, however no clues as to why the golden ants can't be found in other locations nearby.

There was one unfortunate set back at Poochera. Sometime later Dr Bob Taylor gave directions to a Canberra colleague on how to locate to the golden ants. He later got a frantic telephone cool that the site was in chaos, and to drive west immediately.

It was unbelievable. 'Telecom had laid a phone cable through the original grove. They had come down the road verge, found a rock obstruction or some such, taken the cable under the fence, bulldozed our grove, burned the felled trees, buried the cable, and come back onto the road'. Taylor said it was as if the site had been deliberately selected for destruction! It was an accidental disturbance, but even the hardy *Nothomyrmecia* could not cope with disruption on that scale, and sadly there is now one less listed site.

Since the ants were rediscovered in the Poochera area, a further colony has been found by South Australian government entomologists about 150 kilometres to the west near Penong, but Ros told me the golden ants still haven't been found anywhere else in Australia.

The Poocherites became very excited about their 'dinosaur' ants at one point, and there was even talk of building a 'Big Ant', to match the 'Big Galah' down the road and the plethora of big oysters, big prawns, big merinos and big bananas that blight so many towns in the eastern states.

'I heard that the publican damped all that down', said Ros. 'He said he didn't think tourists would pay big money for something like couldn't see except at 3 am on cold nights'.

. . . .

The weather was mercifully cool as we followed the Eyre Highway around the Great Australian Bight, eventually reaching the famous Ninety Mile Straight which runs in a dead-straight line with no curves or bends. There could have been longer stretches when the highway was sealed and re-built in 1976, but the designers deliberately built in curves to try and combat driver fatigue. When the black top was complete from east to west, the following correspondence was noted in the Letters section of the Melbourne *Age* between C A Mullett and U R Fish.

Sir,

few people living in Melbourne this summer could have failed to observe that the tendency of Melbourne's weather to follow that of Perth by a few days as it usually does, has not occurred as it usually does.

I have devoted a considerable time to investigate this phenomenon, discussing it with an applied physicist and other informed people and performing complex meteorological calculations. I have concluded that the root cause for the breakdown in our weather patterns is the recent completion of the bitumen servicing of the Eye Highway across the Nullarbor. The basic mechanism behind this effect revolves around the black-body radiation from the road surface causing thermal updraughts in an unbroken line across the continent…

The obvious solution is to paint the entire surface white to reduce the black body radiation and hence thermal updraughts…

C A Mullett

Sir,

I was most interested in the theory advanced by C A Mullett in his letter (27:1). My interest in the subject stems from my recent doctoral thesis in which I mapped the Nullarbor on a scale of 1:1. As the only place I could lay up my map was naturally enough on the Nullarbor, I had considerable occasion on which to study the Eyre Highway and the black-body phenomenon.

In my opinion Mr Mullett has overlooked too important factors – the curvature of the earth and the speed of weather transfer. The sealing of the Eyre Highway has reduced the weather differential between the two cities to 53.5 hours (a reduction of 4.93 hours)…

The solution is to slow the weather to its former speed by installing 'speed bumps' on the highway... If painted white, these will also break the continuity of the black-body radiation it will be the world's longest pedestrian crossing in the Guinness Book of Records.

U R Fish

Ros saw nothing of the 90 Mile Straight. She fell sound asleep.

. . . .

Ros and I have decided not to drive on to Norseman on the Eyre Highway. We have been told of a more scenic dirt road that can take us more directly down towards Esperance, on the south coast, and as we had an off-road camping outfit, we decided to do that, and make a beeline for the small hamlet of Condingup near the south coast where we could also pick up some fresh supplies and diesel fuel for Penelope.

The God of Camping turned on a short shower of rain as we were packing up to leave the next morning. Just enough to smear mud all over The Manor, and wet the canvas side-walls as they were folded in over our beds.

South of Deralinya Station station the road improved dramatically, particularly when we crossed into the Shire of Esperance. We were back in wheat country for the first time since leaving the far west of South Australia. The vegetation was changing too. The road was lined by a variety of Western Australian Banksia we had not seen before. Both the scrub and cleared farmlands were ablaze with bright yellow flowering trees, known locally is Christmas Bush, or more accurately *Nuytsia floribunda*, named after its discoverer Dutch explorer Pieter Nuyts, who noted it in 1627 while sailing along the south-west coast of Australia.

So in a quest to follow the original explorers of this coast, we are now back in the 17th century. No wonder those who live in the west ponder in some paranoid perplexity about the east-coast delusion that Australian history began with Captain Cook. Pieter Nuyts' Christmas Bush flowers only in December (of course) and is technically a parasite, which overcomes it's grass host proliferating cleared paddocks as well as natural bush. We were right on the button to see its most spectacular display.

The wheat crop was being harvested, and a lumbering road train loomed up ahead, throwing up a great pall of dust. After fifteen minutes or so I became impatient and, as the road was straight, attempted to pass it. As I drew clear of the billowing dust and was able to see dimly, I saw with horror another road train dead ahead, coming straight for us and barely a hundred meters away. I plunged back into the dust, and Ros suggested gently (in a tone of voice she doubtless used in her nursing career to soothe lunatics) that, 'it might be an idea if we stopped by the roadside, had a cup of coffee and let the road trains get well ahead. This was excellent advice. Much better to stop, relax and have a cup of coffee and a biscuit than be dead.

We were heading down to the T-junction with Fisheries Road which runs east from Esperance about thirty kilometres inland from the coast. First though, we turned west for a few kilometres to Condingup to pick up more fuel and fresh supplies. It was the last fuel stop on the Fisheries Road before we reached the coast where we had decided to spend the night at Cape Arid National Park, about a hundred kilometres east of Esperance.

The best the Condingup score could do in the fresh fruit and veggies department was potatoes and onions, but we were pleased to see those – and a packet of frozen meat.

Cape Arid National Park is magnificent. The camping area is divided up into a series of bays among the sand dunes and the brightly flowering Banksias, overlooking the Thomas River inlet and lagoon, with a long curving white beach stretching around the bay towards distant granite promontories. Out to sea the horizon was broken by a number of granite islands, some with vegetation, some without. CALM (the Department of Conservation and Land Management) supplies gas for the barbecue, rough brackish water from a tank on a short tower, and a couple of well-built built toilets, with concrete floors, and plenty of dunny paper. You pay an entrance fee to the park, but camping fees are voluntary.

We had the place to ourselves except for a caravan and an old Toyota four-wheel-drive in the next bay – reminding us that the dreaded school holidays were imminent. As we walked down to the beach to check it out, we passed two small boys returning to their camp, and exchanged a few words. Not long after we expanded The Manor anner into camping mode, the younger of the two boys (he looked about six) arrived with a shy smile and a written invitation to 'Cocktails at six with the Williams – please bring your own glasses'. Well, why not!

Ros discovered that we had had the fridge in The Manor running all day on gas, instead of 12 volt power from the Landcruiser. This was extremely dangerous and naughty, but thankfully all was well. The only minor disaster was leaking beetroot juice, which had escaped from its sealed plastic container and not only permeated every single item in the fridge, but dribbled out the front and formed an obscene, blood like puddle on the floor – also staining a small cotton rug in front of the sink. It was remarkable that it had not reached our beds. One day scientists will discover the mysteries behind the all-pervasive qualities of beetroot juice – how and why it is not only able to insinuate itself through glass and plastic, but also then replicate itself and run wild, staining clothing and all inanimate objects within a square kilometre.

Greg Williams, Heather Messer and the two boys Todd (eight) and Ryan (six) have been on the road for three years! They are from Woolgoolga in New South Wales, and just took off on a working holiday. Neither of the boys has ever been to conventional school. Heather teaches them with help from the New South Wales Distance Education Program. The Williams are also vegetarians. I never thought I'd become emotional about a salad, but when our 'cocktails' drifted seamlessly into a dinner invitation, we crunched happily into lettuce leaves, tomatoes and fresh capsicum. We'd only been on hardtack for less than a week! Heather also had Lebanese hommus dips, black olives and tofu.

Greg is a refrigeration engineer (and jack of many trades by profession) but his real passion is landscape photography, which he hopes one day to practice full time. Meanwhile he works for several months at a time in towns to stock up the family fortunes, then they take to the bush again. They have come to Thomas River for Christmas mostly because of the remoteness and beauty of the place, but also there are no

'Cocktails at Six' at Thomas River, with Heather and Greg and their two small sons. From left: Heather Messer. Todd (8), Ryan (6), Greg Williams and Ros.

Author as Santa with the entire student population of the Coorabie Primary School. Morrie, the owner of the caravan park, had been Santa for many years and all the kids knew this Santa wasn't him. The fact that Morrie was present in the room added to the kids curiosity about my identity. The parental hand (top right) is demanding attention from the moppet on Santa's knee who is more interested in her undelivered present.

camping fees. They are actually doing what many Australians dream of doing but never do.

We form one of those instant accords which can lead to firm friendship (it did!). By the third glass of vino Greg and I were planning a combined expedition to a camping area to the east at Israelite Bay. We will take both Penelope and The Manor while they will leave the caravan at Thomas River and camp in tents from the venerable Toyota Landcruiser. It is always safer to travel with someone, and Greg is one of those handy blokes who can fix anything from a car fridge to a broken axle. Or that's how it seems to me. He's probably got a welding outfit with him as well. I must remember to ask him. After a few more glasses absolutely anything seems possible.

After a head-clearing swim the next morning (even the ultra-dedicated Greg failed to make his customary 5 am photographic foray) we agreed that despite the vinous origins of our enthusiasm the night before, we really would go to Israelite Bay for one or maybe two nights, and began sorting out the gear we would take. The plan was to leave by lunchtime, as the school holiday crowd was expected to descend on Cape Arid within the next two or three days. In fact the outside world started to arrive about ten am that morning when Nissan utility with a strangely familiar white cabin drove past our camp. It had a distinctive stainless steel beer barrel mounted under the rear of the tray. Ros twigged just as the Nissan disappeared around the next corner of the sandy track.

'Tim – it's Ken and Liz from Fowlers Bay!

We had seen them in South Australia at Fowlers Bay, some 150 km west of Ceduna. We had met in a fairly basic caravan park and camping area at Fowlers Bay surrounded by a sheet metal wind break and enjoyed their company very much. I ran after them, but they had spotted us and came back.

. . . .

At Fowlers Bay I had seen Ken's Nissan four-wheel-drive utility looked businesslike, with extra winch cable wound around the front-bull bar. I noticed a stainless-steel beer keg was lying on the rear of the tray – almost certainly for extra water rather than the amber fluid, although Ken is one of those Australians who seems to have a cold beer can in a stubby holder permanently welded into his right hand. Ken looked as durable is his vehicle with an ample belly, splendidly sweat stained, battered Akubra hat with ventilation holes around the crown, and hands and forearms like a navvy. He looked as tough as the proverbial Mallee root. However at the time I thought his greeting a little strange.' Welcome to Fowlers Bay, Santa Claus, would you like some bait'?

By then it was 11 am and already around thirty degrees Centigrade and the tired looking squid, prawns and cockles in his bait bucket were widely advertising their imminent demise in the warm water at the bottom of his bait bucket. But it seemed churlish to refuse. We could see the customary big jetty jutting out into the bay opposite the camping ground, and we had already heard glowing reports of all the fish to be caught at Fowlers Bay. But why is it that whenever we get to a good fishing spot the weather breaks up and tide is wrong? I put the bait in the shade of the sheet metal wind-break, which was the best I could do it that stage.

'What's this Santa business?'

'You'll find out. Which way are you heading?'

'Across to the west.'

'So are we. I'll keep a look out for you.' Ken gunned the motor of the Nissan as he begin to tow the caravan out of the rather stark compound. 'Then I can find out how you got on with the kids...'

A cheery way from Liz and they were gone.

Christmas was still a week away. Ros and I walked along the waterfront to the store with one petrol pump that also doubles the caravan park office. The proprietors Morrie and Margaret were waiting to pounce.

'Thank Gawd, here's Santa at last' – boomed Morrie. 'That other bloke was going to do it, but he shot through. So now you're it'.

I thought Ken had seemed in a hurry. There didn't appear to be any choice in the matter. It turned out that the Coorabie Primary School was having its end of term picnic, and the visit from Santa was the highlight.

'The only trouble is', said Morrie, 'all the kids know me by now, I've done it so many times before. That's why we need you'.

There was time for some fishing from the jetty before I became Mr Ho Ho Ho. In any case, I have to wait for the mail truck to arrive – the far-west substitute for reindeers and a sleigh. The sea-breeze was well and truly in, which didn't do much for the fishing but it least it blew the smell of Ken's ripening bait well away. We tried fishing near the jetty, off the beach, with no luck, so we made the long trek to the end of the jetty where Ros caught a reasonably sized leather-jacket on her first cast. I was struggling with the wind, weed and pessimism. Conditions didn't get any better and the wind got so strong it blew the bucket over, spilling the bait on the planks of the jetty – which was a mixed blessing. We gave it away after an hour and walked back along the jetty to find a small cluster of locals using the very spot that we had tried first. They were hooking portion-sized trevally out of the water with commendable expertise. Must be the way they hold their mouths. The locals I mean.

Morrie was waiting for me at the caravan park with the suitcase. 'Here is the Santa gear, mate. Barry, the mailman is running a bit late, but I've got a message to him to call in here to pick you up, before he goes around to the Community Centre. You'd better get changed, he could be here at any moment. The kids are all down at the beach having a swim. We'll bring them up to the hall as soon as we see the mail truck.'

The Santa kit was impressive, and provided by the Coorabie Primary School. Apart from the red suit (with a big safety pin thoughtfully provided for girth adjustment), there was a long white wig, and impressive beard with moustache attached, and black cloth leggings to simulate boots. A striped pillowslip fleshed out with some empty cardboard boxes completed my ensemble. The Manor provided a little shade, and I stood there waiting for Barry, sweating in full fancy dress except for the red colour fur-trimmed Santa hat which I figured could wait until the last moment. Still, I presented a fairly bizarre sight, and the next two campers to drive into the park clearly thought so too. It could've been one of them instead of me, I brooded…

Half an hour later Barry clattered in the gate with his truck and Morrie materialised with balloons and streamers to tie on the cab. Horn blaring, Santa arrived with much ho ho-ing and excitement. I could see some of the older kids eyeing me off trying to see who I was, but the disguise was perfect. Anyway, there was Morrie in his blue singlet and shorts as large as life among the crowd.

I babbled some nonsense about having broken a runner of the sleigh near Penong on the Eyre Highway and having to hitch a ride with Barry on the mail truck, leaving Dancer and Prancer and Donner and Blitzen with the rest of the reindeers happily eating wheat stubble in the paddock with some sheep.

In the old days Coorabie was a one-teacher school, with all the children catered for in the one classroom. These days there are two teachers, and Santa's flock of about 15 kids ran from pre-school ranging from dribbling toddlers to a startingly tall, bright-eyed Aboriginal girl of about eleven. All sat on Santas knee in their wet bathing suits while I did my best with presents and small talk. I was able to get by with some one-day cricket comments with some of the older boys, but had to fall back on her Ho ho hoing and 'what do you want for Christmas' for the sprogs. With a flash of inspiration I got them all singing 'Jingle Bells', and then ran out of puff. I made a break for the mail truck and got in, but there was no Barry! It was the most protracted goodbye since Melba. I ho hoed away way and waved for what seemed like an eternity before Barry materialised from the shop, kicked his old truck into gear, and delivered a very hot and frazzled Santa with salty damp trousers back to The Manor.

. . . .

As often happens with grey nomads Ken and Liz had coincided with us yet again at Cape Arid National Park. There was the customary 'What have you been doing since… 'and we introduced them to Greg and Heather. Ken materialised with cold beers from the back of his truck and it seemed churlish to refuse. They were camped in their caravan further west and we were exploring the coast.

‘We’re just about to set off to Israelite Bay, said I with the false insouciance of an inexperienced four-wheel-driver. Ken and Liz both shrieked, ‘Are you mad’?

Now Ken is as tough as they get, a South Australian farmer who recently handed over his property to his son to manage, and took to the road for a bit of a break. His Nissan truck has all the four-wheel-drive essentials: Winch, extra wire cable looped along the front of his bull bar, and God knows what else in the back of his cab. If a bush-smart bloke like Ken was spooked by going to Israelite Bay I was ready to listen.

Ken and Liz had set out the previous day. At the end of Fisheries Road, as advertised, the track became four-wheel-drive only. The narrow sand ruts was so deep they could barely see over the banks at either side. Not only that, the sand ruts were ridged with giant corrugations that almost shook their back teeth out.

‘Mate, I’m telling you, it was diabolical. There were tree roots sticking out from the banks on each side of the track that would rip the sides out of your camper tyres. And then we got to the limestone. Fair dinkum, I thought I’d never make it. The point is, we couldn’t have turned back even if we wanted to. So many four-wheel-drives have been through there that the whole road is trenched down about a metre and a half.

‘It took us two hours to go seventeen kilometres. When we got to where we could turn around, we were so buggered we just had a cup of tea and turned around and came straight back.’

Greg Williams was looking thoughtful. I said: ‘What was it like when you go to Israelite Bay’?

‘That was the other thing – bloody awful’. Ken waved his hand towards the glorious beach and blue ocean behind us.’ It’s nothing like this. There are mangroves and bits of scrubby tea tree, and the water is all muddy. Not only that, the four-wheel-drive campers who have been there have left great piles of bottles and garbage behind them. Why would you leave a beaut place like this to go do a dump like that’?

It seemed a pertinent question. Well it was possible Port Malcolm to the south was more attractive, but Liz and Ken was so traumatised by their drive-in to Israelite Bay, that all they wanted to do was to get home.

It's funny how things sometimes work out. If we hadn't met Ken and Liz briefly at Fowlers Bay two weeks before, and if they had driven past a camp in the afternoon rather than the morning, we would've committed ourselves to Israelite Bay and the kind of deeply challenging four-wheel-drive experience we would rather leave to the hardheads.

At least the 'Great Israelite Bay Debate' was finally over. What a relief. We don't have to go! Even a picnic at the dubiously named Poison Creek seemed a better option. But by the time the convoy of three four-wheel-drive vehicles reached the Fisheries Road ready to turn west, Ken and Liz pulled over and stopped. An obscene column of massive smoke was rising into the clear blue sky to the east – from where Ken and Liz calculated they were camped at Duke of Orleans Bay, and said they would head back to check on their caravan. (As it happened the smoke was coming from an offshore – fortunately uninhabited – island that had somehow been set on fire, and the whole island was burnt to a crisp. It looked as if a volcano had erupted.)

Back at camp I was anxious to enlist Greg to get our car fridge working again. The young man in Sydney who installed the twelve volt power outlet in the rear section of Penelope had done so in a way that meant if the fuse ever blew – which it just had –you had to practically demolish the whole side of Penelope to get at it. Well, that is an exaggeration, but to take the side panel out and find the fuse meant dismantling the luggage platform and heavy duty drawers packed with tools, jacks and extra gear. I did the donkey work and Greg was able to fix the fuse and relocated so it could be got at without doing all that ever again. It only seemed to take a minute to fix his brakes. Not being a practical bloke it seemed to me that Greg can fix absolutely anything. We are most grateful. Fancy camping next to a refrigeration engineer!

I found out later that he pumped up the hydraulic pressure on his brake lines with a 50/50 mix of brake fluid and a two dollar bottle of musket we had generously given the Williams (before we realised they were non-drinkers), purchased at a winery near Barmera in South Australia. Six months later the brakes were still working perfectly. Perhaps the winery concerned might like to use it in their advertising.

Over lunch we quizzed Heather and Greg over how they had managed to realise the lifestyle that most couples with young kids only dream about. It all started when Greg and Heather went for a holiday in Sulawesi, Indonesia, in 1994. At that stage Heather was at TAFE teacher working between Grafton and Coffs Harbour, New South Wales, while Greg was managing a wholesale refrigeration and air conditioning business in Coffs Harbour.

'We were also raising two children and trying to owner-build a house', said Greg. 'In words – stress'!

Heather said that the people in the part of Sulawesi where they were holidaying were known as the 'Smiling Minahasens', a name given to them by the colonial Dutch, because of the resilience and good nature of this physically attractive race. During the two-week holiday, Greg and Heather wondered how the Smiling Minahasens could be so happy with so little material wealth. 'Our conclusion was that western society has got it wrong', they said.

Greg's mind was further concentrated by turning forty, 'which made me consider my own mortality and how I could head towards the things I wanted to achieve in life. Sitting at home and wishing I was a great landscape photographer was not the way to achieve my goals.

Heather and Greg had done a round Australia trip in 1988 and were no strangers to camping and travelling. But now they had children who had to be educated. Their family and friends were generally dismissive of their plans.

Heather found a vastly different attitude when she and Greg visited the Distance Education Department at the Casino Public School. 'What struck us was the enthusiasm and acceptance of what we were planning, whereas even our school teacher friends were pessimistic about Todd and Ryan's educational future.

'It was a strange experience to walk into a room where several teachers were having quite animated discussions with invisible students. They were actually making audio tapes to be mailed away to them'.

'Being on the receiving end of this process is virtually a full-time job for Heather. Every week Todd and Ryan each receive a package which has a set period of work, reading material, books and audio tapes, and Heather supervises their daily schooling. But once a week, if possible, the boys talk to other remote area students on a conference phone. Sometimes Greg has to drive them to a mountain top to get reception on his mobile phone.

Both parents are delighted with the way the two boys are progressing. On the their 1998 trip, Greg was appalled at the trouble other travellers went to in order to receive television – even to the extent of having satellite dishes strapped to the back of their caravans.

'One evening I remember Heather, myself and a handful of travellers enjoying a campfire, I lovely chat and a beautiful star-filled sky, while every other caravaner was locked inside getting their hit of television.

Heather and Greg made a deliberate decision not to take a television when they left Woolgoolga, and the boys are essentially growing up without it. This, their parents are convinced, has done wonders for their imagination. Ros and I had noticed their ability to play together happily for hours at a time, using a few stones or shells to augment their toys while chattering away to each other. They seemed to have an instinctive appreciation of the natural surroundings.

Greg said they did go to a formal school for a term while he was working in Perth. On Ryan's first day the eight-year-old chose to eat his lunch up a tree. 'This was not normal and acceptable behaviour, according to the teacher. What crap'!

However at the end of the term Todd's teacher commented that it was refreshing to meet a boy who was untouched by commercialism and obviously spent a lot of time with his father. Greg was delighted.

Heather said that if they wrote a book about their travels it would be called, '*You're So Lucky* – which is what strangers generally said about their lifestyle. But we're not lucky – We just did it'!

. . . .

We kept in touch with Greg and Heather and our friendship has continued to the present day.

12

Losing Ros

I was unaware that Ros was coping with the early symptoms of dementia, but some of her friends noticed changes in her behaviour. She had always been a keen contributor to a book club organised by her women friends in Pacific Palms, Forster and Tuncurry where we had lived since we sold our Sydney home where we had lived for thirty years, (in order to encourage two grown-up sons to leave home).

Ros and I moved into the beach pole-house we had built, first as a weekender, and later our new abode at Boomerang Beach, Pacific Palms, where we lived for the next twenty years.

But by 2016, Ros' book club group noticed that, although she was still attending meetings, she had not often not read the book under discussion and in any case did not want to join in the usual spirited discussions on its merits or failings.

On Friday nights we usually gathered (weather permitting) at Sunset Park on the shores of Wallis Lake in the summer starting at 4 pm where we brought our own drinks, and shared nibbles that were so delicious that any thoughts of a later evening meal were superfluous. If the weather was unfriendly we met in one of our houses. The tradition has been started by long term-Forster residents Rob and Elizabeth Fisher who set up the ground rules including encouraging Sippers members to invite guests from time to time if they wanted to.

Some of the Sippers regulars had noticed Ros' withdrawal from her usual spirited conversations at Sippers, but I was blissfully unaware of any significant changes in Ros' behaviour.

But after a bad fall in North Sydney which had her admitted to North Shore Hospital with a grossly swollen right knee overnight, I began to realise that all was not well with Ros mentally and physically, and she continued to have falls in the garden and even inside our pole house.

Ros with her three grandchildren on her 75th birthday. From left: Abbey Bowden-Grimes, Emily Hennessy-Bowden, Charlie-Hennessy-Bowden.

Ros triumphant with a barramundi caught in the Northern Territory on our last camping trip there in 2007. I caught nothing!

She was diagnosed with Alzheimers in 2017, and it became clear to me that it was not safe for her to live in our pole house with its steep flights of stairs (a belated decision reinforced by local friends) and in March 2019 we put our Boomerang Beach house on the market, which thankfully sold quite quickly, and by August I had made arrangements to lease a two-bedroom flat at Sunrise Supported Living in Tuncurry, which also had nursing back-up, and Ros and I were able to move in by August 2019, where I could be her principal carer.

I mentioned earlier that after we began our married life in New York in 1968, Ros discovered I was a mug with money and took over the family finances. I have had to face up to taking over that role since her dementia took hold, but things are much more simple now we have sold our houses and put most of that into superannuation, and I have a financial adviser now as well to keep me on the straight and narrow.

Ros and I were together at Sunrise for a year until she had an unexpected fall on the concrete of our rear patio in November 2020. Because of the blood thinners she takes for her atrial fibrillation, she developed instant haematomas down her left side and across her back and when we called a doctor he took one look and called an ambulance, which took her to straight to Manning Base Hospital in Taree, about 30 minutes drive from Tuncurry. She was there for five weeks, while experiencing periods of delirium. I received a call from her geriatrician, Dr Nookala, who said: 'I am sorry to say this Tim, but there is no way Ros can return to Sunrise Supported Living as she has to go into a higher level of care'.

Fortuitously there was a spare room in the dementia section of Baptist Care Kularoo Centre in nearby Forster, which has the reputation of being the gold standard in dementia care locally, and she went straight there from Manning Base Hospital where she still is. Happily this is only ten minutes drive from where I continue to live in our unit at Sunrise. I still have dreams that she is still with me and wake to find I am alone in our queen-sized bed. We had been together for 52 years.

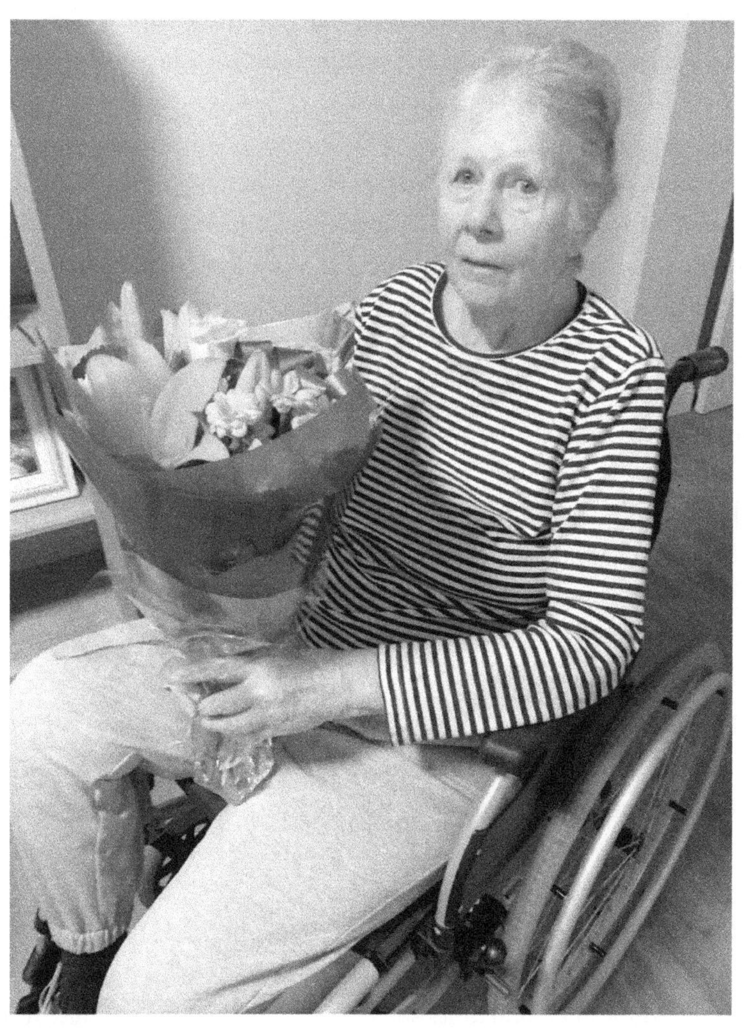

Ros in her room at Baptist Care on her 82nd birthday.

There were some light-hearted moments. About six months ago from the time of writing. I went in to see Ros one morning. During COVID there is a RAT test before you can enter Baptist Care, with cotton swabs up the nose and a 15-minute wait for a negative test. Then you have to be fitted with a white mask over your nose and mouth and go through a com-puter procedure which among other things tests the temperature of your forehead, and puts up questions which have to be answered correctly. At the end it spits out a small sticker, with a black and white postage-stamp-sized image of your face, and your name in very small print which you stick on your jacket front for the time that you are on the premises.

The protocol is that you have to meet with Ros in her room. On this particular day I wondered if she still knew who I was. Out of the blue, I said, 'Who am I Ros'? I had forgotten all about the little ID sticker on my shirt-front.

Now Ros has very good eyesight as she had her cataracts operated on only a few years before. She used to be able to spot dust under a chair in our living room from 20 metres. She peered forwards obviously trying to read the sticker on my chest.

Finally she said', You're Tim Bosun'!

Ah well, a life on the ocean wave…

Up till that time we had been able to have a reasonable conversation during these visits until the relentless progress of this wretched disease produced its next barrier to communication.

It is called 'expressive dysphasia' and works like this. When Ros tries to speak to me, she trips on a plosive consonant and breaks into machine-gun-style stuttering. Sometimes she gets distressed by her inability to talk and shouts gibberish at me non-stop. This is most distressing, and after about 10 minutes of this I alert the staff to the fact that I am leaving, and end my visit.

One way around this is for me to speak in a monologue which does not call for a reply, with news of our sons and their grandchildren. On a recent visit I was rewarded by a small smile at one

one of my jokes. Ros is now in a wheelchair all the time when she is not in bed because of the many falls she had on her knees in the past has made it painful for her to stand or walk. On warm days it is permitted to wheel her outside into grounds of Baptist Care and find a shady spot where I can sit down with her and Ros can take in the flowers and other plants. Alas, not in the winter.

I wrote the first of four travel books following our two-month dash to the south of Western Australia, *Penelope Goes West – On the Road from Sydney to Margaret River and Back*, which was published in 1999, followed by *Penelope Bungles to Broome* (2001), *The Devil in Tim – Penelope's Travels in Tasmania* (2005), and *Down Under in the Top End – Penelope Heads North* (2008). At this point I was politely told by my publisher, Allen & Unwin, that they did not want any more of Penelope's excursions thank you very much.

Not that Ros and I stopped travelling, but it was in the Northern Territory in 2016 that Ros told me that she didn't want to do any more long trips. I was surprised to hear her say that, but acknowledged we had had a fair suck of the proverbial Grey Nomad sauce bottle, and we decided to sell 'The Palace' (The Manor had been upgraded by then). I later realised that this decision was probably a pointer to her developing dementia.

I still find comfort in the memories of the wonderful times we spent together, some of which have been described in this book as well as her adventurous life most of which I have been privileged to share.

www.ingramcontent.com/pod-product-compliance
Lightning Source LLC
Chambersburg PA
CBHW021228090426
42740CB00006B/430

* 9 7 8 1 9 2 2 6 9 8 6 4 3 *